FROM
READING
TO
WRITING

1

LYNN BONESTEEL

Series Editor
LINDA ROBINSON FELLAG

PEARSON
Longman

From Reading to Writing 1

Pearson Education, 10 Bank Street, White Plains, NY 10606

Staff credits: The people who made up the *From Reading to Writing 1* team, representing editorial, production, design, and manufacturing, are Eleanor Barnes, Rosa Chapinal, Dave Dickey, Oliva Fernandez, Françoise Leffler, Massimo Rubini, Jennifer Stem, Jane Townsend, Paula Van Ells, and Patricia Wosczyk.

Text composition: ElectraGraphics, Inc.
Text font: 11 pt New Aster
Photo credits: See page 173.

Library of Congress Cataloging-in-Publication Data
Bonesteel, Lynn.
    From reading to writing / Lynn Bonesteel . . . [et al.].
        p. cm.
    Includes index.
    ISBN 0-13-205066-8—ISBN 0-13-612780-0—ISBN 0-13-233096-2—
ISBN 0-13-158867-2 1. English language—Textbooks for foreign
speakers. 2. Reading comprehension—Problems, exercises, etc. I.
Title.
    PE1128.B6223 2010
    428.2'4—dc22

                                                                    2009032265

ISBN-13: 978-0-13-205066-1 (with ProofWriter™)
ISBN-10: 0-13-205066-8 (with ProofWriter™)

ISBN-13: 978-0-13-247402-3 (without ProofWriter™)
ISBN-10: 0-13-247402-6 (without ProofWriter™)

PEARSON LONGMAN ON THE **WEB**

Pearsonlongman.com offers online resources for teachers and students. Access our Companion Websites, our online catalog, and our local offices around the world.

Visit us at **pearsonlongman.com**.

ISBN: 0-13-205066-8 (with ProofWriter™)

ISBN: 0-13-247402-6 (without ProofWriter™)   11 17

Printed in the United States of America

Contents

Introduction   v
Scope and Sequence   x

UNIT ONE   Around the World   1

Chapter 1   Cultural Rules   2
Chapter 2   The Land of Smiles   12

UNIT TWO   A Special Animal   21

Chapter 3   Four Animals or One?   22
Chapter 4   The Beautiful Stranger   32

UNIT THREE   The Art and Science of Food   41

Chapter 5   Science in the Kitchen   42
Chapter 6   The Art of Food   52

UNIT FOUR   Memory   61

Chapter 7   Memory Methods   62
Chapter 8   Smell, Memory, and Sales   72

UNIT FIVE   **Housing**   81

    Chapter 9   Cohousing   82

    Chapter 10   The Micro-Compact Home   92

UNIT SIX   **The Art of Medicine**   101

    Chapter 11   One Doctor, One Patient,
        Two Different Worlds   102

    Chapter 12   An Artist and a Doctor   112

UNIT SEVEN   **The Working World**   121

    Chapter 13   Doing Business in the United Kingdom   122

    Chapter 14   E-Mail: Terrific Tool or Time-Waster?   131

UNIT EIGHT   **What's Next?**   141

    Chapter 15   Is 50 the New 30, and 70 the New 50?   142

    Chapter 16   Millennials in the Workforce   151

Grammar Reference   161

Punctuation and Capitalization   166

Editing Symbols   168

Target Vocabulary   169

Sources   171

Photo Credits   173

Index   175

Introduction

From Reading to Writing 1 is the first in a four-book series that integrates reading and writing skills and strategies for English language learners. The four-book series includes:

Book 1—Beginning Level

Book 2—High Beginning Level

Book 3—Intermediate Level

Book 4—High Intermediate Level

Reciprocal Reading/Writing Integration

From Reading to Writing provides a complete sequence of high-interest, thematically connected activities that reciprocally integrate reading and writing.

- Students build competence in vocabulary and reading as they move toward writing skill development and completion of a writing assignment.
- Students study the features and language of reading texts, and learn to apply them in their own writing.
- In the same way, writing is integrated into the reading process in accordance with research that suggests writing can enhance reading comprehension (Mlynarcyzk, Spack).

Books 1–3 contain eight thematically focused units. Each unit consists of two topically related chapters, divided into two main sections— Reading and Writing—which are linked by a bridge section. Book 4 is organized into nine units. Each unit consists of two thematically connected readings that have accompanying skills and practice activities and are linked by a bridge section, From Reading to Writing. Each reading is also followed by a writing section.

Books 1–3

Each chapter in Books 1–3 includes:

Pre-Reading
Discussion
Vocabulary

Reading
Identifying Main Ideas and Details, Making Inferences
Reading Skill and Practice

Bridge Section—From Reading to Writing
Discussion, Vocabulary Review, Journal Writing

Writing
Writing Model or Examples
Writing Skills and Practice
Writing Assignment
Writing Process Steps

Book 4

Each unit of Book 4 includes:

Pre-Reading 1
Discussion
Vocabulary

Reading 1
Identifying Main Ideas and Details, Making Inferences
Reading and Vocabulary Skill and Practice

Bridge Section—From Reading to Writing
Discussion and Journal Writing

Pre-Reading 2
Discussion
Vocabulary

Reading 2
Identifying Main Ideas and Details, Making Inferences

Writing
Writing Model
Writing Skills and Practice
Writing Assignment
Writing Process Steps

Detailed Explanation of Parts, Books 1–3

Part 1, Reading

In the Pre-Reading section, students build schema by discussing the theme and studying key vocabulary before reading. High-interest readings and lively activities engage students as they develop vocabulary and reading skills and strategies that can be used in their own writing.

Bridge Section—From Reading to Writing

The Reflecting on the Reading activity focuses on content from the reading and how it can be applied to student writing. In some levels, a journal activity provides an opportunity for freewriting. Students can use target vocabulary and explore a question from the reflection activity in depth. Some levels also include exercises to activate vocabulary. Students are asked questions using target vocabulary and are encouraged to use their answers in the upcoming writing assignment.

Part 2, Writing

Writing models and examples as well as writing skills practice allow students to hone their writing skills before they produce their own writing. In the writing assignment, students are led step-by-step through the writing process. This encourages them to gather ideas, focus and organize, and revise and edit their writing. This step-by-step process facilitates collaboration with classmates and the instructor and also promotes self-evaluation of writing.

Benefits to Students

This sequence of activities, common to Books 1–3, has at its core a set of essential competencies for pre-academic English learners that are emphasized throughout the four-book series. Upon completion of the activities, students will be prepared to:

- Recognize and produce a variety of sentences to express ideas (Books 1–2)
- Recognize and utilize the steps in the writing process to produce a composition (Books 2–4)
- Use ideas and language gained from reading in writing and speaking (Books 1–4)

- Organize and write a composition with a main idea and supporting ideas (Books 1–4)

- Recognize and use connectors and other devices that show relationships among ideas in texts (Books 1–4)

- Recognize and express the main idea and supporting details of a reading (Books 1–4)

Vocabulary Focus

The *From Reading to Writing* series also features a strong focus on vocabulary development. The high-frequency vocabulary targeted in each book is derived from three highly recognized vocabulary lists:
- West's *General Service List* (1953) of the 2,000 most frequently used words in English
- Coxhead's *Academic Word List* (2000) of the 570 most common word families
- Dilin Liu's list of most common idioms (2003)

Vocabulary experts agree that academic-bound students who acquire the words on the West and Coxhead lists will know more than 90 percent of the words they will encounter in academic texts (Nation, 2000). Furthermore, research studies have shown that repeated exposure to new words, and application of new vocabulary in writing and speech, increase the chances that students will acquire the target words (N. Schmitt, Nation, Laufer).

From Reading to Writing stresses vocabulary acquisition by providing opportunities for students to encounter, study, and use new words in each of these sections of a chapter or unit:
- Pre-Reading vocabulary activities
- Reading
- Post-Reading vocabulary review
- From Reading to Writing bridge section

Writing Resources

A full complement of appendices serve as resources for student writers. These include a Grammar Reference; a Punctuation and Capitalization section; an Editing Symbols chart, which presents commonly used editing marks, and an alphabetized word list of Target Vocabulary, organized by unit. Additionally, an online e-rater lets students submit their compositions and receive prompt, individualized feedback.

References

Coxhead, A. (2000). "A New Academic Word List." *TESOL Quarterly*, 34(2), 213–38.

Laufer, B. (2003). "Vocabulary Acquisition in a Second Language: Do Learners Really Acquire Most Vocabulary by Reading?" *Canadian Modern Language Review* 59, 4: 565–585.

Liu, Dilin. (2003). "The Most Frequently Used Spoken American English Idioms: A Corpus Analysis and Its Implications." *TESOL Quarterly* 37, 671–700.

Mlynarcyzk, Rebecca. (1993). "Conversations of the Mind: A Study of the Reading/Writing Journals of Bilingual College Students." Diss. New York U, *DAI* 54, 4004A.

Nation, I. S. P. (2001). *Learning Vocabulary in Another Language.* Cambridge: Cambridge University Press.

Schmitt, N. (2000). *Vocabulary in Language Teaching.* Cambridge: Cambridge University Press.

Schmitt, N. & McCarthy, M. (Eds.). (1997). *Vocabulary: Description, Acquisition, and Pedagogy.* Cambridge: Cambridge University Press.

Spack, Ruth. (1993). "Student Meets Text, Text Meets Student: Finding a Way into Academic Discourse." *Reading in the Composition Classroom: Second Language Perspectives.* Joan G. Carson and Ilona Leki (Eds.). Boston: Heinle, 183–96.

Scope and Sequence

Unit		Reading	Reading Skills	Verb Tense Used	Writing Skills	Writing Assignment
1	Around the World	Chapter 1 *Cultural Rules*	Finding the topic of a paragraph	Multiple	• Writing a complete sentence • Using correct punctuation for sentences	Write individual sentences following prompts
		Chapter 2 *The Land of Smiles*			Using correct word order	Write individual sentences following prompts
2	A Special Animal	Chapter 3 *Four Animals or One?*	Identifying main ideas	• Simple present • Simple past of *be*	Making subjects and verbs agree	Write individual sentences
		Chapter 4 *The Beautiful Stranger*			Using capital letters	Write individual sentences
3	The Art and Science of Food	Chapter 5 *Science in the Kitchen*	Finding supporting sentences	• Simple present • Present continuous	Writing compound sentences with *and* and *but*	Write individual compound sentences
		Chapter 6 *The Art of Food*			• Formatting a paragraph • Writing compound sentences with *so* and *or*	Write individual compound sentences in paragraph form
4	Memory	Chapter 7 *Memory Methods*	Understanding pronoun reference	Simple past	Using pronouns	Write individual sentences with pronouns in paragraph form
		Chapter 8 *Smell, Memory, and Sales*			Using present time and past time together	Write a paragraph showing both present time and past time

Unit		Reading	Reading Skills	Verb Tense Used	Writing Skills	Writing Assignment
5	Housing	Chapter 9 *Cohousing*	Identifying topic sentences	Simple past	• Using *There is / There are* • Replacing *There is / There are* with pronouns	Write a paragraph with *There is / There are*
		Chapter 10 *The Micro-Compact Home*			Using descriptive adjectives	Write a paragraph about a place
6	The Art of Medicine	Chapter 11 *One Doctor, One Patient, Two Different Worlds*	Understanding time order	Simple past	Using time clauses	Write a paragraph about an experience
		Chapter 12 *An Artist and a Doctor*			Using prepositional phrases of time	Write a paragraph about the life of an interesting person
7	The Working World	Chapter 13 *Doing Business in the United Kingdom*	Understanding signal words	*Can* and imperative	Using the imperative	Write a paragraph that gives advice
		Chapter 14 *E-Mail: Terrific Tool or Time-Waster?*			Using signal words	Write a paragraph that explains how to do something
8	What's Next?	Chapter 15 *Is 50 the New 30, and 70 the New 50?*	Understanding cause and effect	Future tense	Using *because* and *so*	Write an opinion paragraph
		Chapter 16 *Millennials in the Workforce*			• Using future time clauses • Using clauses with *if*	Write a paragraph about future plans

UNIT ONE

Around the World

Cultural Rules

*In this chapter
you will:*

• read about
cultural rules

• learn to find
the topic of
a paragraph

• write complete
sentences

PRE-READING

Discussion

Discuss the questions in pairs or small groups.

1. Look at the picture. What do you see? Where are the people?
   What is happening?
2. In your culture, how do young people greet (say hello to) the
   elderly people in their family?
3. In your culture, how do young people greet elderly people they
   don't know or don't know very well?

Vocabulary

A. Read the sentences. Match the boldfaced words with the definitions in the box.

_c_ 1. I don't know how to play. Can you explain the **rules** to me?

____ 2. Can we leave? I'm the only woman at the party. I feel very **uncomfortable**.

____ 3. You made a lot of **mistakes** on the test. You need to study more or you're going to fail the course.

____ 4. My grandfather is 80 years old. He is a quiet, kind person. All of his grandchildren **respect** him.

> a. admire someone and have a good opinion of him or her
> b. a little bit worried or embarrassed
> c. things that you can or cannot do in certain situations, for example in a game or in a new culture
> d. things that are not correct

B. Read the sentences. Match the boldfaced words with the definitions in the box.

____ 1. It is raining a lot. Please drive **carefully**.

____ 2. Don't **touch** the window with your dirty hands!

____ 3. Most men don't cry **in public**, but they sometimes cry when they are alone.

____ 4. In many cultures, it is not **acceptable** to put your feet up on a table.

> a. put your finger, hand, etc., on something or someone
> b. correct or good for a particular situation
> c. (done) in a way that shows you are thinking about what you are doing, so that you do not cause something bad to happen
> d. in a place where other people can see or hear

Cultural Rules

1   It is very interesting to meet people from other cultures. But what do we do when we meet them? Do we shake hands or kiss? Do we look into their eyes? Every culture has different **rules** about **touching** and eye contact.[1] What are the rules? How do we learn them?

2   When, where, and how do people touch? The rules are very different from culture to culture. It is easy to make a **mistake** and do something that is not **acceptable**. In some cultures, for example Japan, most people don't touch **in public**. In South Korea, men and women don't touch, but women often hold hands. In Brazil, people say hello with a kiss. To learn the rules, watch people **carefully**, and ask questions. And if you are not sure, don't touch!

3   Eye contact is also important in every culture. In some parts of Africa, you look down to show that you **respect** someone. But in North America, you look people in the eye[2] to show that you respect them. In most of North and South America, when a speaker talks to a large group, people look at the speaker. This shows they are listening. In the same situation, the Japanese sometimes close their eyes. They say it helps them listen.

4   How can you learn the rules of eye contact? First of all, if you are talking and the other person looks **uncomfortable**, think about why. It might be your eye contact. Also, watch what native speakers do. But don't stare![3] Staring is almost never acceptable.

5   These days, we often meet people from different cultures. Of course, we will never learn the rules of every culture. We will also make many mistakes. We need to accept that. But we can watch carefully, ask questions, and learn from our mistakes.

---

[1] **eye contact:** When you make eye contact with someone, you look into the person's eyes.
[2] **look someone in the eye:** look directly into someone's eyes
[3] **stare:** look at someone or something for a long time without moving your eyes

Identifying Main Ideas

What is the reading about? Circle the letter of the best answer.

a. Rules about touching and eye contact are important in every culture.
b. You will make mistakes when you visit other cultures.
c. People from different cultures should not touch each other.

Identifying Details

Complete the sentences with names of places from the reading.

1. Most people do not touch in public in _____Japan_____ .

2. Women often hold hands in _____.

3. People kiss when they say hello in _____.

4. People look down to show respect in _____.

5. People from _____ usually look you in the eye when they talk to you.

6. People look at the speaker to show that they are listening in _____.

7. Some people close their eyes when they listen to a speaker in _____.

READING SKILL

Finding the Topic of a Paragraph

A paragraph is a **group of sentences**. A paragraph has just **one topic**. When we start a new topic, we start a new paragraph. We show that a group of sentences is a paragraph by **indenting** (leaving the first five spaces blank), like this:

INDENT 5 SPACES

  When, where, and how do people touch? The rules are very different from culture to culture. It is easy to make a mistake and do something that is not acceptable. In some cultures, for example Japan, most people don't touch in public. In South Korea, men and women don't touch, but women often hold hands. In Brazil, people say hello with a kiss. To learn the rules, watch people carefully, and ask questions. And if you are not sure, don't touch!

To find the topic of a paragraph, ask: *Who or what is the paragraph about?* The topic of paragraph 2 in the reading is *the rules of touching in different cultures*.

Practice

A. Look at the reading. What is the topic of paragraph 3? Check (✔) the correct answer.

_____ 1. how to show that you are listening

_____ 2. eye contact in Africa

_____ 3. why eye contact is important

B. Read the paragraph. What is the topic? Check (✔) the correct answer.

People from different cultures greet each other in different ways. When you visit another culture, it is important to learn the correct way to greet someone. In some countries, for example China, people do not touch or kiss when they greet each other. They just smile and say hello. In other cultures, for example Saudi Arabia, men kiss men, and women kiss women, but men and women never kiss in public. In fact, they don't touch at all. They don't look each other in the eye, either. It is always a good idea to learn about acceptable greetings before you travel to another country.

____ 1. visiting another country

____ 2. how men and women greet each other

____ 3. the way people greet in different cultures

FROM READING TO WRITING

Reflecting on the Reading

Discuss the questions with your classmates.

1. In your culture, is it acceptable to touch other people in public?
   - Do husbands and wives touch?
   - Do friends touch?
   - Do teachers touch children?
   - Do people touch when they meet for the first time?

2. In your culture, is it acceptable to make eye contact in these situations?
   - You are walking down the street, and someone you don't know is coming toward you.
   - You are listening to the teacher in class.
   - The teacher asks you a question, and you don't know the answer.
   - Your boss is angry with you because you made a mistake.

Activating Your Vocabulary

Complete the sentences with the words from the box.

acceptable	in public	respect	~~touch~~
carefully	mistake	rules	uncomfortable

1. In some cultures, you should not _____*touch*_____ someone on the head.

2. In many parts of Europe, young people hold hands and kiss _____.

3. In Saudi Arabia, it is never _____ for a man to touch a woman who is not from his family.

4. When you visit another culture, you should _____ the people and their customs.

5. If you make a _____, say that you are sorry.

6. You can learn a lot about a culture if you watch and listen _____.

7. We all feel _____ when we do something wrong in another culture.

8. Before you visit another country, try to learn some of the _____ and customs.

In Japan, people bow to greet each other.

WRITING
SKILL

Writing a Complete Sentence

Every sentence needs a subject and a verb. The **subject** is a person, animal, place, or thing. The subject can be a noun, for example, *woman*, or a pronoun, for example, *she*. The subject comes before the verb. The **verb** describes an action (for example, *meet*) or a state or condition (for example, *be* or *feel*).

EXAMPLES

SUBJECT   VERB
- **We meet** people from other cultures.

SUBJECT   VERB
- **The rules are** different.

SUBJECT   VERB
- **That isn't** the rule in my culture.

Practice

A. Read the sentences. Underline the subjects and circle the verbs.

1. People don't touch in public.

2. Women hold hands.

3. People look at the speaker.

4. Men and women don't touch.

5. Cultures have different rules.

6. Eye contact is important.

7. This is acceptable.

8. They feel uncomfortable.

9. Some people shake hands.

10. The Japanese bow.

B. **Read the paragraph. Underline the subjects and circle the verbs.**

Many languages (have) a special word for *teacher*. Students in those countries call their teachers *teacher*. They do not call them by their name. This shows their respect. In other languages, students call their teachers by name. In their culture, this shows respect. For example, American children use their teacher's last name with *Mr.* or *Ms.* in front of it. College students sometimes use their professors' first names.

READING SKILL

Using Correct Punctuation for Sentences

Sentences start with a **capital letter** and end with a **period (.)** or a **question mark (?)**. We use a period for statements and a question mark for questions.

EXAMPLES

CAPITAL LETTER   PERIOD

- It is easy to make a mistake.

CAPITAL LETTER   QUESTION MARK

- Which rules are most important?

Editing

Add capital letters and a period or a question mark to the sentences.

1. ͲThe rules are very different from culture to culture⊙

2. when, where, and how do people touch

3. in Brazil, people say hello with a kiss

4. how can you learn the rules of eye contact

5. it might be your eye contact

6. we need to accept that

Write sentences about rules for touching and eye contact in your culture. Follow the steps.

STEP 1   **Get ideas.**

Work in pairs. Ask and answer the questions. If you don't know a word, check your dictionary or ask someone the meaning.

1. What country are you from?
2. How do people greet each other? Do they touch? For example, do they shake hands? Do they bow? Do they kiss? Do they hug?
3. Do people in your country touch in public?
4. Are the rules about touching in public the same for men and women? For example, do men touch men? Do women touch women? Do men and women touch?
5. Do people in your culture use a lot of eye contact?
6. When do people in your culture use eye contact? For example, do they look at each other in elevators or on a bus or subway?

STEP 2   **Write sentences.**

Write six sentences about your culture. Use information from your conversation with your partner.

1. _____

2. _____

3. _____

4. _____

5. _____

6. _____

STEP 3   **Check your work.**

Read your sentences. Use the writing checklist to look for mistakes, and use the editing symbols on page 168 to mark corrections.

> ### Writing Checklist
> ❏ Does every sentence begin with a capital letter?
> ❏ Does every sentence end with a period?
> ❏ Does every sentence have a subject?
> ❏ Does every sentence have a verb?

STEP 4   **Write a final copy.**

Correct your mistakes. Write a final copy of your sentences and give it to your instructor.

The Land of Smiles

In this chapter you will:

• read about a country where smiling is very important

• learn about correct sentence order

• write sentences with subjects, verbs, and objects

PRE-READING

Discussion

Discuss the questions in pairs or small groups.

1. Look at the picture. What country do you think the people are from? Why are they smiling?
2. Do you know of any places where people smile a lot? Do you know of any places where people *don't* smile a lot? What are the places?
3. Do you know anyone who smiles a lot? Do you know anyone who almost never smiles? Who are they?

Vocabulary

**A. Read the boldfaced words and their definitions. Then complete each
sentence with the correct word.**

> **agree:** If you agree with someone, you think that what he
> or she says is right.
> **face:** the front of your head, with your eyes, nose, and
> mouth
> **funny:** If something is funny, it makes you laugh.
> **relationship:** the way in which two people or groups feel and
> behave toward each other

1. Why are you laughing? Did someone say something ____*funny*____?

2. Wash your _____ and hands. They are dirty.

3. The _____ between a mother and child is very special.

4. He says that boys shouldn't cry, but I don't _____.
   These days, I think it's acceptable for boys to cry.

**B. Read the boldfaced words and their definitions. Then complete each
sentence with the correct word.**

> **especially:** used to say that something is more true of one
> person or thing than of other people or things
> **expression:** the look on someone's face
> **notice:** see, feel, or hear someone or something interesting
> or unusual
> **owe:** have to pay money to someone because you
> borrowed it from him or her

1. He's not sad. He's happy. Look at his _____.

2. You should always drive carefully, but it is _____
   important when the weather is bad.

3. We can't go out to dinner. We don't have any money. We
   _____ $1,000 on our credit card.

4. I love nice clothes. I always _____ the clothes that
   people are wearing.

The Land of Smiles

1   Thai people smile a lot. Most visitors to Thailand **notice** that right away.[1] In fact, Thailand is called "The Land of Smiles." The Thai word for smiling is *yim*. There are many different kinds of *yim*. For each kind of *yim*, Thais use a different **expression** on their **faces**. It shows the meaning of the smile. In his book on Thailand, *Working with the Thais*, Henry Holmes names 13 different kinds of smiles. Thais use most of them every day.

2   Thais often smile in uncomfortable or difficult situations. They think that smiling is **especially** important then. It keeps **relationships** between people strong. There are many different kinds of smiles for difficult situations. One of them means "I don't **agree** with you" (*yim thak thaan*). Another one means "I know the situation is bad, but there's no point in crying[2] about it now"(*yim yae-yae*). Then there's the smile that means "I know I **owe** you money, but I don't have it" (*yim haeng*). There's even a smile for jokes[3] that aren't **funny** (*fuen yim*)!

3   Of course Thais also smile in happy or friendly situations. But there are only a few kinds of smiles for these situations. One of them means "I'm so happy I'm crying" (*yim thang nam taa*). Thais use it when they are very very happy. Another one means "I respect you" (*yim cheun chom*). Finally, there is the smile for people you don't know (*yim thak thaii*).

4   In all cultures, people smile when they are happy. And people from many cultures smile in difficult situations. But in the Land of Smiles, there is a smile for almost every situation.

....
[1]**right away:** very quickly
[2]**there's no point in crying:** crying will not help the situation
[3]**joke:** something funny that you say to make people laugh

Identifying Main Ideas

Read each question. Circle the letter of the best answer.

1. What is the topic of the reading?
   a. Thai people smile all the time because they are very happy.
   b. In the Thai language, there are 13 different words for *smile*.
   c. Thai people have many different kinds of smiles for different situations.

2. What is the topic of paragraph 2?

   a. smiles for important relationships

   b. smiles for difficult situations

   c. smiles for mistakes

3. What is the topic of paragraph 3?

   a. smiles for happy situations

   b. smiles for respect

   c. smiles for new friends

Identifying Details

Complete each sentence. Circle the letter of the best answer.

1. The word for *smile* in Thai is _____.

   a. *yim*   b. *fuen yim*   c. *yim haeng*

2. Henry Holmes wrote a book about _____.

   a. smiling   b. Thailand   c. funny situations

3. The text explains the meaning of _____ different kinds of smiles in Thailand.

   a. 13   b. 7   c. 5

4. _____ is *not* in the text.

   a. The "I respect you" smile

   b. The "Your joke isn't funny" smile

   c. The "I agree" smile

FROM READING TO WRITING

Reflecting on the Reading

Check (✔) your answers to the questions. Then discuss your answers in pairs or small groups.

1. Most people in my culture smile _____.

   ____ a. a lot

   ____ b. a little

(continued)

2. Most people in my culture smile _____.

_____ **a.** in difficult or uncomfortable situations

_____ **b.** in sad situations

_____ **c.** in funny situations

3. People in my culture *don't* usually smile _____.

_____ **a.** in difficult or uncomfortable situations

_____ **b.** in sad situations

_____ **c.** in funny situations

Activating Your Vocabulary

Complete each sentence. Circle the letter of the best answer.

1. In my culture, the expression on his face means that he is _____.

   (**a.**) angry   **b.** dirty

2. I agree with you. I think you're _____.

   a. right   **b.** wrong

3. People from that culture are very funny. They like to _____.

   a. work   **b.** laugh

4. Smiling is especially _____ in Thai culture.

   a. difficult   **b.** important

5. Why are you _____? You owe a lot of money!

   a. smiling   **b.** unhappy

6. Here, relationships are important. We _____ other people.

   a. dislike   **b.** need

7. The first thing people notice about him is his nose. It is _____.

   a. large   **b.** on his face

8. I think Alexandra is _____ here. She always has a big smile on her face.

   a. happy   **b.** angry

**WRITING
SKILL**

Using Correct Word Order

Many sentences in English follow this order:

SUBJECT VERB OBJECT

• People visit Thailand.

You learned that every sentence needs a subject and a verb. Some verbs also need an **object**. Objects come after the verb. Subjects and objects are **nouns** or **pronouns**. Nouns and pronouns name people, animals, places, and things.

EXAMPLES

NOUN   NOUN

• **Visitors** like **Thailand**.

PRONOUN PRONOUN

• **They** like **it**.

Practice

A. Read each sentence. Underline the subject once and the object twice. Circle the verb.

1. <u>Visitors</u> (notice) <u><u>the Thai smile</u></u>.

2. Thais use many different facial expressions.

3. He owes money.

4. Our faces show our feelings.

5. Babies touch their mother's faces.

6. Different cultures have different rules.

7. The teacher respects her students.

8. The teacher never hits her students.

9. She touched him.

10. They greeted their friends.

B. Complete the paragraph with the words from the box.

Nouns	Verbs
expressions	tell
feelings	~~use~~
People	watch
	words

People in all cultures (1) _____*use*_____ their faces and their words to talk. Facial (2) _____ are very important. Our faces show our (3) _____. (4) _____ often say one thing with their faces and a completely different thing with their (5) _____. I (6) _____ people's faces carefully. Their expressions usually (7) _____ the truth.

WRITING ASSIGNMENT

Write sentences about your country and the people. Follow the steps.

STEP 1   Get ideas.

Work in pairs. Ask and answer the questions. If you don't know a word, check your dictionary or ask someone the meaning.

1. What is special about your country? What do visitors to your country notice about it?
2. What do you like about your country or the people from your country?
3. What don't you like about your country or the people from your country?
4. Do people in your country usually talk about their feelings? Do they show their feelings on their faces?
5. Do most people in your country use their hands and bodies when they talk?
6. Do people in your culture smile a lot?

STEP 2   Write sentences.

Write six sentences about your country and the people. Use information from your conversation with your partner.

1. _____

2. _____

3. _____

4. _____

5. _____

6. _____

STEP 3   Check your work.

Read your sentences. Use the writing checklist to look for mistakes, and use the editing symbols on page 168 to mark corrections.

> ### Writing Checklist
> ❑ Does every sentence begin with a capital letter and end with a period?
> ❑ Does every sentence have a subject and a verb?
> ❑ Do some of your sentences have objects?
> ❑ Are the subjects, verbs, and objects in the correct order?
> ❑ Are the subjects and objects nouns or pronouns?

STEP 4   Write a final copy.

Correct your mistakes. Write a final copy of your sentences and give it to your instructor.

UNIT TWO

A Special Animal

Four Animals or One?

In this chapter you will:

• read about an interesting animal

• learn about main ideas in readings

• write sentences with correct subject and verb agreement

PRE-READING

Discussion

Discuss the questions in pairs or small groups.

1. Look at the picture. Match the body parts with the words. Write the correct number next to each word.

   ____ **a.** ear   ____ **c.** eye   ____ **e.** eyelashes
   ____ **b.** neck   ____ **d.** tongue

2. Look at the animals on page 21. Do you know the names of the animals in English? Match the names in the box to the pictures.

camel	cow	giraffe	leopard	snake

3. Which of the words describe a giraffe? Which describe a leopard? Write *G* for giraffe and *L* for leopard. If a word describes both, write *GL*. Then compare your answers.

_____ a. tall   _____ d. beautiful   _____ g. scary
_____ b. sweet   _____ e. strong   _____ h. smart
_____ c. strange   _____ f. fast

Vocabulary

A. Read the sentences. Match the boldfaced words with the definitions in the box.

_b_ 1. In soccer, players **kick** the ball. They don't touch it with their hands.

_____ 2. **Danger**! Do not enter. This is a one-way street.

_____ 3. You need to **protect** your eyes from the sun. Here are some sunglasses.

_____ 4. Dogs and cats are both animals, but they have very different **characteristics**.

> a. a possibility that something or someone will get hurt
> b. hit someone or something with the foot
> c. things that make one animal, person, or thing different from another
> d. keep someone or something safe

B. Read the sentences. Match the boldfaced words with the definitions in the box.

_____ 1. I didn't sleep well. The bed was too **hard**.

_____ 2. Cats usually run away and **hide** from dogs.

_____ 3. It is difficult to cut her hair. It is very **thick**.

_____ 4. Our cat has two white **spots** on her head.

> a. go somewhere where others cannot see or find you
> b. not soft
> c. small marks or areas of color that are a different color from the area around them
> d. growing very close together without much space in between

Four Animals or One?

1   When you look at a giraffe, what do you see? Some people see the **characteristics** of four animals: a leopard's coat, a camel's head and neck, a cow's feet, and a snake for a tongue. Why does the giraffe have so many different characteristics? The giraffe needs all of its characteristics to survive.[1]

2   Giraffes are very tall and have long necks for two reasons. First, they eat from the tops of very tall trees. Second, they need to see over the tops of the trees. They can see danger, like a lion, from far away. Then they have time to run away or **hide**.

3   The giraffe's coat is also important to its survival. It has brown **spots** and is very **thick**. The spots help the giraffe hide among the trees. The giraffe's thick coat **protects** it from the sun.

4   Two other important characteristics of the giraffe are its large eyes and long, thick eyelashes. With its large eyes it can see very well. The eyelashes protect its eyes. The giraffe sees better than most other large animals in Africa.

5   A giraffe's feet and legs are also important characteristics. The giraffe uses them for protection. It has **hard** feet, like a cow. It also has very strong legs. If a lion comes too close, the giraffe can **kick** it in the head. That usually kills the lion.

6   One last characteristic is the giraffe's long black tongue. It is about 18 inches long. With their tongues, giraffes get food far above their heads. They also clean their eyes and ears with their tongues. Why is the giraffe's tongue black? The color protects it from the sun.

7   Maybe the giraffe looks like four animals, but of course we know that it is not. It is one animal, with many different characteristics. Its characteristics help it survive.

....

[1] **survive:** continue to live, especially in difficult or dangerous conditions

Identifying Main Ideas

A. What is the reading about? Check (✔) the best answer.

_____ 1. Giraffes, camels, and cows look the same.

_____ 2. Giraffes have the characteristics of many different animals.

_____ 3. Giraffes' special characteristics help them survive.

B. Match the topics to the paragraphs in the reading. Write the number of the paragraph next to its topic.

__2__ 1. why the giraffe is tall with a long neck

_____ 2. the giraffe's tongue

_____ 3. the eyes of the giraffe

_____ 4. the coat of the giraffe

_____ 5. the giraffe's feet and legs

Identifying Details

Mark each sentence T (true) or F (false). Then correct each false sentence to make it true.

__F__ 1. The giraffe's tongue looks like a ~~cow's tongue~~. *snake*

_____ 2. Giraffes use their long necks and tongues to get food.

_____ 3. Giraffes eat food from the ground.

_____ 4. Giraffes can see very far because they are tall and their eyes are large.

_____ 5. The giraffe's coat is very hot.

_____ 6. Giraffes cannot hide among the trees.

_____ 7. Sometimes giraffes kill lions.

_____ 8. Giraffes' feet are soft.

_____ 9. Giraffes clean their coats with their tongues.

_____ 10. The giraffe's tongue is long.

Identifying Main Ideas

Every reading has a main idea. The main idea includes the topic of the reading and the writer's idea, opinion, or feeling about the topic. When a reading has more than one paragraph, the main-idea sentence is often at the end of the first paragraph. Look at the example—main-idea sentence from "Four Animals or One?"

EXAMPLE

┌── TOPIC ──┐ ┌──────── WRITER'S IDEA ABOUT THE TOPIC ────────┐
- **The giraffe** needs all of its characteristics to survive.
└────────────────────── MAIN IDEA ──────────────────────┘

Paragraphs also need main ideas. The main-idea sentence of a paragraph is often the first sentence of the paragraph.

Practice

A. Read each main-idea sentence. Circle the topic. Underline the writer's idea about the topic.

1. (Zoos) teach children to respect animals.

2. Animals in zoos have terrible lives.

3. The giraffe is the most beautiful animal in Africa

4. Lions are dangerous animals.

5. My trip to Africa changed my life.

6. Animals need protection from people.

7. Cats are excellent pets.

8. Pets are good for children.

9. Dogs are man's best friend.

10. My children love animals.

11. Some pets have better lives than people.

12. Snakes are very interesting.

B. *Each paragraph needs a main-idea sentence. Read the paragraph and circle the letter of the best choice.*

1. _____. When a giraffe is born, it falls on its head. But the 6-foot fall does not hurt it at all. About an hour later, the baby stands up and walks for the first time. Sometimes the mother leaves the new baby alone for most of the day, but it doesn't cry. It just sits alone and waits for its mother to come back.

   a. From the time they are born, baby giraffes are strong.

   b. A baby giraffe is similar to the babies of many other animals.

   c. Baby giraffes need their mothers to survive.

2. _____. I was five years old, and my mother took me to the zoo for my birthday. When we drove into the parking lot, I saw the head of an animal. It was looking at us over the top of some trees. I was very scared, so my mother took me home. We never went into the zoo that day. I had bad dreams about that giraffe for months.

   a. My mother always took me to a special place for my birthday.

   b. Giraffes are the most interesting animals in the zoo.

   c. I will never forget the first time I saw a giraffe.

3. _____. They are strange and beautiful. They are very friendly and sweet. They look at you with their big eyes. They eat peanuts from your hands with their long black tongues. Their mouths are soft, like a horse's mouth. If you are lucky, they will give you a kiss!

   a. The giraffes at the zoo eat out of your hands.

   b. Giraffes are my favorite animals to visit at the city zoo.

   c. Giraffes and horses are very similar.

FROM READING TO WRITING

Reflecting on the Reading

Discuss the questions in pairs or small groups.

1. Do you like to learn about animals? Why or why not?
2. What is your favorite animal? Why is it your favorite?
3. What animals don't you like? Why don't you like them?

Activating Your Vocabulary

Complete the sentences below with the words from the box.

~~characteristics~~	hard	kick	spots
danger	hide	protect	thick

1. Giraffes have many interesting *characteristics*.
2. The _____ on a giraffe's coat are usually dark brown.
3. Sometimes giraffes _____ among the trees. That way, lions can't find them.
4. A giraffe has _____ feet. It can hurt or even kill a lion with its feet.
5. When a giraffe sees _____, it can run away.
6. Giraffes have _____ coats and eyelashes.
7. A giraffe's legs are very strong. It can _____ a lion in the head and kill it.
8. Mother giraffes _____ their babies from lions.

WRITING

WRITING SKILL

Making Subjects and Verbs Agree

You have learned that every sentence needs a subject and a verb. The form of the verb needs to agree with, or match, the subject. In the sentences below, the **subjects and verbs agree in number**. A singular subject (only one thing) needs one kind of verb. A plural subject (more than one thing) needs another kind of verb.

EXAMPLES

SUBJECT VERB
- **The coat is** thick.

SUBJECT VERB
- **It protects** the giraffe from the sun.

SUBJECT VERB
- **Giraffes are** very tall.

SUBJECT VERB
- **They eat** from the tops of very tall trees.

The subject is a person, place, or thing. Sometimes **other words come before or after the subject**. These words may describe the subject or the verb, but they do not change the verb. **The verb always agrees with the subject.**

EXAMPLES

SUBJECT VERB
- The giraffe's **coat is** thick.

SUBJECT VERB
- The giraffe's **eyes are** very large.

SUBJECT   VERB
- Maybe **the color protects** it from the sun.

Practice

A. Underline the subject. Then circle the verb form that agrees with the subject.

1. Their eyelashes **is** / **are** long and thick.

2. The eyelashes **protects** / **protect** its eyes.

3. The giraffe **sees** / **see** better than most other large animals.

4. It **has** / **have** brown spots.

5. Giraffes **has** / **have** hard feet.

6. The color **protects** / **protect** it from the sun.

B. Read each sentence. Underline the subject and circle the verb. Correct any verb that doesn't agree with its subject.

get
1. With their tongues, giraffes gets food far above their heads.

2. Two important characteristics are its large eyes and long, thick eyelashes.

3. With its large eyes, it see very well.

4. A giraffe's feet and legs are also important characteristics.

5. It also have very strong legs.

6. First, they eats from the tops of very tall trees.

Editing

Read the paragraph. Correct the capitalization and punctuation, and fix the mistakes in subject-verb agreement. There are six mistakes including the examples.

        is

The giraffe ~~are~~ a beautiful and special animal. ~~i~~**I**t have spots all over its body The spots on its coat is usually brown. The eyes of the giraffe are amazing. They are soft and warm With its beautiful eyes and coat, the giraffe is a very special animal.

WRITING ASSIGNMENT

Write sentences about an interesting animal. Follow the steps.

STEP 1   **Get ideas.**

Work in pairs. Ask and answer the questions. If you don't know a word, use your dictionary or ask someone the meaning.

1. What is the name of the animal? Where does it live?
2. How big is your animal? How tall is it?
3. What special characteristics does it have? For example, what color is its coat? Does it have spots? How big are its eyes?
4. Which characteristics protect your animal? How?
5. What is it like? Is it dangerous? Is it intelligent?
6. What else is important or interesting about your animal?

STEP 2 **Write sentences.**

Write six sentences about your animal. Use information from your conversation with your partner.

1. _____

2. _____

3. _____

4. _____

5. _____

6. _____

STEP 3 **Check your work.**

Read your sentences. Use the writing checklist to look for mistakes, and use the editing symbols on page 168 to mark corrections.

Writing Checklist

❑ Does every sentence begin with a capital letter and end with a period?

❑ Does every sentence have a subject and a verb?

❑ Do the subjects and the verbs agree?

STEP 4 **Write a final copy.**

Correct your mistakes. Write a final copy of your sentences and give it to your instructor.

The Beautiful Stranger

*In this chapter
you will:*

• read a story
about a famous
animal

• learn about
noun and verb
forms of words

• write sentences
using capital
letters correctly

PRE-READING

Discussion

Discuss the questions in pairs or small groups.

1. Look at the picture. What animal do you see?
2. What is unusual about the picture?
3. The story you are going to read really happened. What do you
   think happened in the story? When and where did it happen?

Vocabulary

A. Read the sentences. Match the boldfaced words with the definitions in the box.

_d_ 1. Did the plane **arrive** on time?

____ 2. Your daughter is very pretty. I am sure that she will be a great **beauty** one day.

____ 3. Please visit our country. We **welcome** all visitors.

____ 4. She isn't from around here. I'm not sure what her name is. She is a **stranger**.

> a. someone you do not know
> b. say hello in a friendly way to someone to make him or her feel comfortable
> c. something or someone that is very nice to look at
> d. get to a place

B. Read the boldfaced words and their definitions. Then complete each sentence with the correct word.

> **gift:** something that you give to someone, usually for a special reason
> **spend:** use a period of time doing something (past = _spent_)
> **popular:** liked by a lot of people
> **famous:** known and admired by a lot of people

1. Pablo Picasso is a _____ painter. People all over the world know his name and can recognize his paintings.

2. Blue is a _____ color. Many people like it.

3. We have a two-week vacation. We're going to _____ one week in Boston and one week in New York.

4. I get a _____ every year on my birthday from my mother. Usually she gives me clothes.

The Beautiful Stranger

1   In October, 1826, a ship **arrived** in Marseille, France. On the ship was a very special visitor. She had a long neck, large dark eyes, thick eyelashes, and a beautiful spotted coat. When the French **welcomed** her, they named her "The Beautiful **Stranger**." But this **beauty** was not a woman. She was the first giraffe to visit France.

2   How did a giraffe get from her home in Africa to France? She was a **gift** from Egypt to King Charles X of France. She traveled on a boat more than 2,000 miles down the Nile River to Alexandria, Egypt. Then she traveled by ship across the Mediterranean Sea to France.

3   After her arrival in France, the giraffe walked from Marseille to Paris. It was a long walk—550 miles! Thousands of people came out to welcome her. She needed a lot of milk every day, so cows traveled with her at all times. In one town, a French woman made a special raincoat for her. It protected the giraffe from bad weather. She also wore a necklace[1] from Egypt around her long neck. It protected her from danger.

4   By the end of her long walk, the giraffe wasn't a stranger anymore. She was **famous**. Everyone in France knew and loved her. Women wanted necklaces like hers. Men wore tall hats *à la girafe*. They named new colors after her, such as "Giraffe in Love." Clothes of these colors became very **popular**.

5   The giraffe **spent** the rest of her life in Paris. She lived in a special house in the king's garden. She welcomed thousands of visitors there. She was very popular. Many years after she died, people still talked about the tall beauty from Egypt.

---

[1] **necklace**: a piece of jewelry that you wear around your neck

Identifying Main Ideas

A. What is the main idea of the reading? Check (✔) the best answer.

____ 1. The first giraffe to visit France became famous.

____ 2. The giraffe was a gift from Egypt to France.

____ 3. The giraffe's trip to France was difficult.

B. Match the topics to paragraphs 2, 3, 4, and 5 in the reading. Write the number of the paragraph next to its topic.

_5_ 1. life in Paris

____ 2. the trip from Africa to France

____ 3. from strange to famous

____ 4. the walk to Paris

Identifying Details

Complete each sentence. Circle the letter of the correct answer.

1. The giraffe was a gift from _____.
   a. Egypt to France
   b. France to Egypt
   c. the people of France to King Charles X

2. The giraffe traveled to Alexandria _____.
   a. with the king of France
   b. in a raincoat
   c. on a boat

3. The first French city that the giraffe visited was _____.
   a. Marseille
   b. Paris
   c. Alexandria

4. The giraffe walked from _____.
   a. Alexandria to Marseille
   b. Marseille to Paris
   c. Paris to Egypt

5. The giraffe had _____.
   a. a hat *à la girafe*
   b. a raincoat and a necklace
   c. a new color

6. The giraffe _____.
   a. did not like visitors
   b. died in Africa
   c. lived in the king's garden

Reflecting on the Reading

Discuss the questions in pairs or small groups.

1. In your opinion, why did the leader of Egypt give the king of France a giraffe as a gift? Was it a good gift? Why or why not?
2. The Beautiful Stranger became very famous in France. Do you know about any other famous animals? Why are they famous?
3. Do people ever give animals as gifts in your culture? If so, what kinds of animals?

Activating Your Vocabulary

Complete the sentences with the words from the box.

arrived	famous	popular	stranger
beauty	~~gift~~	spend	welcome

1. France did not buy the giraffe. She was a _____*gift*_____ from Egypt.

2. The French people were happy to _____ the giraffe to their country. Thousands of people came out to see her on her walk from Marseille to Paris.

3. The French loved to look at the giraffe. They wanted to dress like her because she was a _____!

4. The giraffe was not _____ when she first got to France. People didn't know about her.

5. Necklaces like the giraffe's became very _____. Women all over France wore them.

6. Before the giraffe _____ in Paris, she walked more than 500 miles.

7. The giraffe was born in Africa, but she did not _____ her life there. She lived in France for more than half of her life.

8. When the giraffe first came to France, she was a _____. Nobody knew her.

WRITING

WRITING SKILL

Using Capital Letters

You learned that the first word in a sentence always begins with a capital letter. In addition, **some nouns always begin with a capital letter**, even if they are not the first word in the sentence. They are called **proper nouns**.

EXAMPLES

- *People's names:* Jill Jones
- *Titles:* Dr., Mr., Mrs., Ms., Miss
- *Rivers, lakes, mountains:* the Nile
- *Continents:* Africa
- *Cities and countries:* Paris, France
- *Nationalities:* Egyptian
- *Languages:* French, Arabic

- *Days of the week:* Monday
- *Months of the year:* January
- *Holidays:* New Year's Day
- *The pronoun* I

We use capital letters only with proper nouns.

EXAMPLES

- The Nile River is long.
- The river is long.

Practice

Add capital letters and a period or question mark to each sentence. Then find each sentence in the reading on page 34 and check your work.

1. in october, 1826, a ship arrived in marseille, france

2. how did a giraffe get from her home in africa to france

3. she was a gift from egypt to king charles X of france

4. she traveled on a boat more than 2,000 miles down the nile river to alexandria, egypt

5. after her arrival in france, the giraffe walked from marseille to paris

Editing

Read the paragraph. Correct the capitalization mistakes. There are six mistakes including the example.

   I

in the past, World leaders sometimes gave gifts of animals or plants

to other leaders. For example, in 1826 muhammed Ali of Egypt gave

King Charles X a Giraffe. Today animals are not common gifts, but

sometimes leaders give trees. as an example, canada gives a Christmas

tree to the city of Boston every year.

WRITING ASSIGNMENT

Write sentences about pets or zoos. Follow the steps.

STEP 1 **Get ideas.**

Work in pairs. Choose a topic. Ask and answer the questions. If you
don't know a word, check your dictionary or ask someone the meaning.

❑ **Topic 1:** Pets in your country

1. Are pets popular in your country?
2. What kinds of pets do people in your country have?
3. Where do people in your country get pets? For example, do they
   buy them? Do they get them as gifts? Do they find them?
4. In your opinion, what kinds of animals are good pets for children?
   Why are they good pets for children?
5. What kinds of animals are good pets for adults? Why are they
   good pets for adults?

❑ **Topic 2:** Zoos in your country

1. Are zoos popular in your country? Who likes to visit zoos?
2. What kinds of animals do the zoos in your country have?
3. Do the animals have a lot of space to move around?
4. Do you like to visit zoos? Why or why not?
5. If you like to visit zoos, what is your favorite animal in the zoo?
   Why is it your favorite?

STEP 2 **Write sentences.**

Write six sentences about your topic. Use information from your conversation with your partner.

1. _____

2. _____

3. _____

4. _____

5. _____

6. _____

STEP 3 **Check your work.**

Read your sentences. Use the writing checklist to look for mistakes, and use the editing symbols on page 168 to mark corrections.

Writing Checklist

❑ Does every sentence begin with a capital letter and end with a period?

❑ Does every sentence have a subject and a verb?

❑ Do the subjects and the verbs agree?

❑ Did you use capital letters correctly?

STEP 4 **Write a final copy.**

Correct your mistakes. Write a final copy of your sentences and give it to your instructor.

The Art and Science of Food

Henri Matisse, The Red Room, *1908*

Science in the Kitchen

PRE-READING

Discussion

Discuss the questions in pairs or small groups.

1. Look at the picture. What is happening? What do you think is wrong with the soup?
2. Check (✓) the kinds of food that you like. Put an *X* next to the foods you do not like. If you don't know a word, ask a classmate or look in your dictionary.

____ bread	____ ice cream	____ soup
____ cake and cookies	____ meat	____ vegetables
____ fish	____ pasta	
____ fruit	____ rice	

Vocabulary

A. Read the sentences. Match the boldfaced words with the definitions in the box.

_b_ 1. This **dish** is delicious! You're a great cook!

___ 2. **Taste** this. Do you think it needs more salt?

___ 3. Don't touch the stove. You'll **burn** your hand.

___ 4. This fruit isn't **ripe**. It's hard. We can't eat it yet.

a. hurt your body with fire or something hot
b. food that you prepare in a particular way
c. ripe fruit is ready to be eaten
d. put a small amount of food or drink in your mouth in order to find out what it is like

B. Read the sentences. Match the boldfaced words with the definitions in the box.

___ 1. The food in my country is **spicy**. We use a lot of hot peppers when we cook.

___ 2. Julia never puts sugar in her coffee. She doesn't like her coffee to be **sweet**.

___ 3. There are some good **recipes** in this cookbook.

___ 4. Let's have ice cream for **dessert**.

a. sugary food that you eat after the main part of the meal
b. a set of instructions that tells you how to cook something
c. having a special taste that comes from plants
d. containing sugar or tasting like sugar

Science in the Kitchen

1   It's 5:00, and your parents are arriving for dinner at 6:00. It's their first visit to your home, and you're cooking a delicious dinner. Everything is perfect . . . until you **taste** the soup. It's too salty! No one will want to eat it! Every cook makes this same mistake at one time or another. Is there anything you can do when you make a mistake like this? If you understand a little about the science of food and cooking, you will find the answers to some of your problems in the kitchen.

2   First of all, let's see if science can help our cook with the salty soup. If you put too much salt in a **dish**, there are a couple of things that you can try. Cut a potato into two pieces, and add it to the soup. The potato will absorb[1] some of the salt, and then you can take it out. You can also add something **sweet**, like sugar, to the soup. It won't take the salt away, but the sweetness will make the taste of the soup less salty. But be careful! Don't add too much sugar, or the soup will taste like **dessert**.

3   Speaking of dessert, what if the fruit you bought for dessert isn't **ripe**? Is there anything you can do? Yes, there is. There is one way to ripen fruit faster. You will need a very ripe banana, with brown spots on it. Why? There is a gas[2] that comes from ripe bananas. That gas makes fruit ripen faster. If you put the dessert fruit in a paper bag with the ripe banana, soon it will be ripe.

4   Finally, a lot of popular **recipes** these days have chili peppers in them. Chili peppers make food taste good, but you need to be careful when you cook with them. Some chili peppers are very strong. They can make the food too hot to eat. They can also make your mouth feel like it is **burning**. So how can you use chili peppers when you cook? Many people cut out the seeds[3] of the peppers. They believe that the seeds make the peppers hot, but that is not true. The soft, white part under the seeds is the hot part. You need to cut out both the white part of the chili pepper and the seeds. If the dish is already cooked and it's too **spicy**, add cream or yogurt[4] to it. Why? The fat[5] in yogurt and cream will stop the burning.

5   All cooks make mistakes. The difference between a good cook and a bad one is often just a little science. And if science can't help, there's always that little restaurant down the street!

----

[1] **absorb:** if something absorbs liquid, it takes it in and holds it
[2] **gas:** something such as air that is not liquid or solid, and usually can't be seen
[3] **seed:** the small part of a plant that a new plant grows from
[4] **yogurt:** a smooth, thick liquid food made from milk
[5] **fat:** something oily that comes from certain animals and plants (cheese, milk, and most meat have fat in them)

Identifying Main Ideas

Read each question. Circle the letter of the best answer.

1. What is the main idea of the reading?
   a. Everything is perfect . . . until you taste the soup.
   b. Every cook makes this same mistake at one time or another.
   c. If you understand a little about the science of food and cooking, you will find the answers to some of your problems in the kitchen.

2. Which sentence is the main-idea sentence of paragraph 2?
   a. If you put too much salt in a dish, there are a couple of things that you can try.
   b. It won't take the salt away, but the sweetness will make the soup taste less salty.

3. Which sentence is the main-idea sentence of paragraph 3?
   a. There is a gas that comes from ripe bananas.
   b. There is one way to make fruit ripen faster.

4. Which sentence is the main-idea sentence of paragraph 4?
   a. Chili peppers make food taste good, but you need to be careful when you cook with them.
   b. Some chili peppers are very strong.

Identifying Details

Match each solution in the box to a problem. Be careful. One of the problems has more than one solution.

Add some yogurt.	Put it in a bag with a ripe banana.
~~Add a little sugar.~~	Put a potato into the dish.

PROBLEM	SOLUTION
1. Your dish is too salty.	*Add a little sugar.*
2. Your dish is too spicy.	
3. The fruit isn't ripe.	

Finding Supporting Sentences

You learned that the main idea of a reading includes the topic and the writer's idea, opinion, or feeling about the topic. Other sentences in the reading give more specific information about the main idea. They are called supporting sentences. **Supporting sentences explain or prove the main idea** with examples, facts, and reasons.

EXAMPLES

- My favorite dish from my country is quesadillas. (*main idea*)
- I like them because they're easy to make. (*supporting sentence*)
- I also like them because they're delicious. (*supporting sentence*)

Practice

A. Read each pair of sentences. Write an M next to the sentence that gives the main idea. Write an S next to the sentence that supports the main idea.

1. _S_ **a.** In Louisiana, many popular dishes have cooked tomatoes in them.

   _M_ **b.** In different parts of the United States, different dishes are popular.

2. ____ **a.** The food in Texas is very similar to Mexican food.

   ____ **b.** Texas is very close to Mexico, and many Texans come from Mexico.

3. ____ **a.** I eat vegetables almost every day.

   ____ **b.** I love vegetables.

4. ____ **a.** Fast food has a lot of fat and salt in it, and salt and fat are not good for you.

   ____ **b.** You should not eat too much fast food.

B. Read each main-idea sentence. Check (✓) the sentence that supports the main idea.

1. Cooking is an excellent hobby.

   ____ **a.** It is fun.

   ____ **b.** It is expensive.

2. Good food is important to a good life.

   ____ **a.** I eat a lot of fast food.

   ____ **b.** People who eat well feel better.

3. It is easy to cook good food these days.

    ____ **a.** There are a lot of good recipes on the Internet.

    ____ **b.** Men and women like to cook.

4. It is difficult to cook for one person.

    ____ **a.** It is not fun to eat in a restaurant alone.

    ____ **b.** Most recipes are for four to six people.

FROM READING TO WRITING

Reflecting on the Reading

Discuss the questions in pairs or small groups.

1. Do you know how to cook? What can you cook?
2. Who cooks the most in your house? Is he or she a good cook?
3. How often do you eat at home? How often do you eat out?

Activating Your Vocabulary

Complete the sentences with the words from the box.

burned	dish	ripe	sweet
~~dessert~~	recipe	spicy	tastes

1. What do you want for _____*dessert*____? I have ice cream, cookies, or cake.

2. This milk _____ strange. I think it's old.

3. Ouch! The soup is so hot, I _____ my tongue.

4. The bananas aren't _____ yet, but I think they'll be ready to eat tomorrow.

5. Don't order that dish if you don't like hot peppers. It's very

    _____.

6. We only make this _____ once a year.

7. I don't like food that is very _____. That's why I don't like cakes, cookies, and chocolate.

8. I made the cake from an old family _____. I got it from my grandmother.

Writing Compound Sentences with *and* and *but*

Simple sentences usually have one subject and one verb. When you join two simple sentences together with **and** or **but**, you get a **compound sentence**. Put a **comma (,)** before the *and* or *but*.

EXAMPLES

SIMPLE SENTENCES

- It's 5:00. Your husband's parents are arriving for dinner at 6:00.
- It won't take the salt away. It will make the taste of the soup less salty.

COMPOUND SENTENCES

- It's 5:00, **and** your husband's parents are arriving for dinner at 6:00.
- It won't take the salt away, **but** it will make the taste of the soup less salty.

Use **and** when the idea in the second sentence **adds information** to the first idea.

Use **but** when the idea in the second sentence **shows a contrast**, or a difference, from the idea in the first sentence.

Practice

A. Complete each sentence with and or but.

1. I love good food, ___*but*___ I'm not a very good cook.
2. This soup is too salty, _____ it's cold. I can't eat it.
3. The fruit looks good, _____ it isn't ripe.
4. We were on time for dinner, _____ the dinner wasn't ready.
5. Chili peppers are delicious, _____ they are good for you.
6. The food was terrible, _____ the waiter was slow. I'll never go to that restaurant again.
7. The bananas are ripe, _____ the other fruit is not ready to eat.
8. The food looks beautiful, _____ it tastes great.
9. The chef burned the meat, _____ the dessert was very good.
10. He's a good cook, _____ usually he doesn't have time to cook.
11. His desserts are great, _____ they are not too sweet.
12. I have a great recipe for banana cake, _____ I don't have any bananas!

B. Combine each pair of simple sentences to make one compound sentence. Use and or but. Add a comma (,).

1. You are planning on fruit for dessert. It isn't ripe.

   You are planning on fruit for dessert, but it isn't ripe.

2. Put the fruit in a bag. Add a ripe banana.

   Put the fruit in a bag, and add a ripe banana.

3. The other fruit will ripen nicely. The banana won't be good to eat.

   _____

4. Cut a potato into two pieces. Put it in the soup.

   _____

5. The soup is good. It needs more salt.

   _____

6. I made a mistake with the recipe. Everyone loved the dish.

   _____

7. My husband loves fish. My son hates it.

   _____

8. I hate cooking. I am not very interested in food.

   _____

9. The soup is cold. The bread is old.

   _____

10. It's my favorite restaurant. I don't go there very often.

   _____

Editing

Read the paragraph. Correct the use of and and but, and fix the mistakes in punctuation and capitalization. There are six mistakes including the examples.

It is easy to be a great cook these days. ~~y~~^You can learn from the best
chefs in the world. Many of their recipes are on the Internet, ~~but~~ *and* some
chefs have their own cooking shows on television In the past, People
paid a lot of money to learn the secrets of great chefs, and today you
can get their secrets for free. Just turn on your television or computer,
And start cooking!

Write sentences about a dish from your country. Follow the steps.

STEP 1   Get ideas.

Work in pairs. Ask and answer the questions. If you don't know a word, check your dictionary or ask someone the meaning.

1. What is the name of the dish?
2. What does it have in it? For example, does it have meat? What kind of meat? Does it have vegetables? What kinds of vegetables?
3. How does it taste? Is it spicy? Is it sweet? Is it salty?
4. Is it difficult to make? Do you know how to make it?
5. When do people eat it? For example, do they eat it every week or only on special days?

STEP 2   Write sentences.

Write five sentences about your dish. One or two of them should be compound sentences with *and* or *but*. Use information from your conversation with your partner.

1. _____

   _____

2. _____

   _____

3. _____

   _____

4. _____

   _____

5. _____

   _____

STEP 3 Check your work.

Read your sentences. Use the writing checklist to look for mistakes, and use the editing symbols on page 168 to make corrections.

> ### Writing Checklist
>
> ❑ Does every sentence begin with a capital letter and end with a period?
>
> ❑ Does every sentence have a subject and a verb?
>
> ❑ Do the subjects and the verbs agree?
>
> ❑ Did you use some compound sentences?
>
> ❑ Did you use *and* and *but* correctly in the compound sentences?

STEP 4 Write a final copy.

Correct your mistakes. Write a final copy of your sentences and give it to your instructor.

The Art of Food

PRE-READING

Discussion

Discuss the questions in pairs or small groups.

1. Look at the picture. Would you like to eat this dish? Why or why not?
2. Read the following sentence, and talk about what it means.
   "We eat with our eyes."
   Do you think it is true?

Vocabulary

A. Read the boldfaced words and their definitions. Then complete each sentence with the correct word.

attractive:	pretty or nice to look at
fill:	put something in a container or space so that it becomes full
fortunately:	happening because of good luck
prevent:	stop something from happening, or stop someone from doing something

1. First, _____ *fill* _____ the pot with water. Heat the water until it boils. Then add the vegetables.

2. When I fry eggs, the butter in the pan always burns. How can I _____ the butter from burning?

3. She isn't a beauty like her sister, but she is very _____.

4. Their house burned down in a fire. They lost everything, but _____, no one was hurt.

B. Read the boldfaced words and their definitions. Then complete each sentence with the correct word.

meal:	the food that you eat at a particular time
reheat:	make something hot again after it has become cold
serve:	give someone food or drinks as a part of breakfast, lunch, or dinner
variety:	a lot of different (things)

1. Cooks make the food, but waiters _____ it.

2. There is some soup from last night in the refrigerator. You can _____ it in the microwave.

3. I like my son to eat a _____ of food. It's not good for him to eat the same thing every day.

4. In my country, lunch is the most important _____ of the day.

The Art of Food

1   We look at our food before we taste it. That's why we often say that we eat with our eyes. Chefs in good restaurants know this, so they are very careful about how their food looks. But you don't need to go to expensive restaurants to eat **attractive** food. You can do some very easy things at home to make your **meals** look as good as they taste.

2   Let's start with something very simple, like cooking an egg. When you boil[1] an egg, it often breaks open, and part of the egg comes out of the shell.[2] This doesn't look very attractive. **Fortunately**, it's easy to **prevent**. Before you put the egg in the water, make a small hole in one end with a pin.[3] Your shells will never crack[4] again!

3   Vegetables are a part of most meals, but often their colors change after they are cooked. To prevent this, always wait for the water to boil. Then add the vegetables. While they are boiling, **fill** a large bowl with ice water. After the vegetables are cooked, put them into the ice water. This stops the cooking before their colors change. Then you can **reheat** them, and they won't lose their color.

4   Color is important for everything you **serve**. It is important to have a **variety** of colors on the plate. For example, if the food on a plate is all white, such as white potatoes, white fish, and white cauliflower, it is not attractive to most people. Try to have three or more colors on the plate at every meal.

5   Taste is very important, but good food is more than just taste. Food needs to look attractive, or no one will want to eat it. Fortunately, there are many simple things you can do to make meals beautiful to the mouth *and* to the eye.

----

[1]**boil:** if a liquid boils, it gets very hot and produces bubbles and steam
[2]**shell:** the hard outer part that protects nuts, eggs, seeds, and some types of animals
[3]**pin:** a short, very thin piece of metal with a sharp point
[4]**crack:** if something cracks, it breaks so that it gets a line on its surface

Identifying Main Ideas

A. What is the main idea of the reading? Check (✔) the best answer.

_____ 1. We look at our food before we taste it.

_____ 2. Chefs in good restaurants know this, so they are very careful about how their food looks.

_____ 3. You can do some very easy things at home to make your meals look as good as they taste.

B. **Read each sentence below from the reading. Write M *if it is a main-idea sentence. Write* S *if it is a supporting sentence.***

  M   1. Let's start with something very simple, like cooking an egg.

_____ 2. Before you put the egg in the water, make a small hole in one end with a pin.

_____ 3. Vegetables are a part of most meals, but often their colors change after they are cooked.

_____ 4. While they are boiling, fill a large bowl with ice water.

_____ 5. Color is important for everything you serve.

_____ 6. Fortunately, there are many simple things that you can do to make meals beautiful to the mouth *and* to the eye.

Identifying Details

Complete each sentence. Circle the letter of the best answer.

1. To prevent egg shells from cracking, _____.
    a. boil the water before you put the eggs in
    b. make a hole in one end of the egg

2. To prevent cooked vegetables from changing color, _____.
    a. put them in ice water after they are cooked
    b. put them in ice water before you cook them

3. To make your meals look attractive, _____.
    a. use recipes from famous chefs
    b. put food of different colors on one plate

FROM READING TO WRITING

Reflecting on the Reading

Discuss the questions in pairs or small groups.

1. What other things do cooks do to make food look attractive?
2. Think of an attractive dish from your country. What is the name of the dish? What makes it attractive? Describe it to your classmates.
3. What is your favorite dish? Why do you like it so much? Is it because it looks attractive?

Activating Your Vocabulary

Complete each sentence. Circle the letter of the best answer.

1. This dish is delicious, but it isn't very _____. You should be more careful about the way the food looks.

   a. salty   **(b.)** attractive

2. Fortunately, everyone was _____, so I had extra time to finish cooking.

   a. early   **b.** late

3. _____ is an example of a meal.

   a. dinner   **b.** dessert

4. If you want to _____ an accident in the kitchen, never leave the room when something is cooking on the stove.

   a. reheat   **b.** prevent

5. I love the _____ in this supermarket. They always have something new.

   a. variety   **b.** dish

6. You need to reheat this before you eat it. It's _____.

   a. cold   **b.** hot

7. At most _____, nobody serves you. You serve yourself.

   a. expensive restaurants   **b.** fast-food restaurants

8. Please fill the sugar bowl. There _____ sugar in it.

   a. isn't much   **b.** is a lot of

WRITING

Formatting a Paragraph

When you write a paragraph, it is important to use the correct form. Follow these steps:

1. Indent the first sentence by leaving five blank spaces before the first word.
2. Write your second sentence immediately after the first. Do not start a new line for every sentence. Keep writing to the right margin.
3. You can start a sentence on one line and finish it on the next line.

Read the model paragraph. Look carefully at its form.

MODEL

WRITE TO RIGHT MARGIN

INDENT   START NEXT SENTENCE ON SAME LINE

I love to cook, so I decided to open a restaurant. I didn't have a lot of money, but I had a big dream. Everyone in my family helped me. My younger brother washed dishes, and my older brother served the food. My mother did something different every night. She helped me in the kitchen, or she helped my brother in the dining room. She even washed dishes sometimes. The first year was very difficult, so I was lucky to have my family's help.

START SENTENCE ON ONE LINE AND FINISH ON ANOTHER

Writing Compound Sentences with *so* and *or*

You have learned about compound sentences with *and* and *but*. You can also make **compound sentences** with *so* and *or*.

Use *so* when the idea in the first clause is the cause or reason and the idea in the second clause is the result or effect.

EXAMPLE

CAUSE OR REASON   RESULT OR EFFECT

- Chefs want food to look attractive, **so** they use a variety of colors.

Use *or* when the idea in the first clause is one possibility or choice, and the idea in the second clause is a different possibility or choice.

EXAMPLE

ONE POSSIBILITY OR CHOICE   ANOTHER POSSIBILITY OR CHOICE

- Food needs to look attractive, **or** no one will want to eat it.

Practice

A. Complete each sentence with so or or.

1. The food looked terrible, ___*so*___ no one wanted to eat it.

2. I made a small hole in the eggshell, _____ it didn't crack.

3. Make a hole in the eggshell, _____ it will crack.

4. She wants to be a chef, _____ she is going to cooking school.

5. Her dishes need to look attractive, _____ she will never be a great chef.

B. Combine each pair of simple sentences to make one compound sentence. Use so or or. Don't forget to add a comma (,).

1. Don't use food of just one color. The dish won't be attractive.

    Don't use food of just one color, or the dish won't be attractive.

2. Boil the water first. The vegetables will lose their color.

    _____

3. I put the cooked vegetables into ice water. They didn't lose their color.

    _____

4. There was a variety of different-colored food on the table. It looked very attractive.

    _____

5. That chef serves beautiful and delicious food. His restaurant is very popular.

    _____

6. Use ripe fruit. The dessert won't taste good.

    _____

WRITING ASSIGNMENT

Write a paragraph about a great restaurant. You can write about a real restaurant, or you can imagine one. Follow the steps.

STEP 1   **Get ideas.**

Work in pairs. Ask and answer the questions. If you don't know a word, check your dictionary or ask someone the meaning.

1. What is the name of the restaurant?
2. Where is it?
3. What kind of restaurant is it? What kinds of food do they serve?
4. What does the restaurant look like? For example, is it big or small? Is it formal or casual?
5. Is it an expensive restaurant? How much do the main dishes cost? How much do the desserts cost?
6. What is the chef's best dish?

STEP 2   **Write sentences.**

Write sentences about your restaurant. Answer the questions above in order. Use some simple sentences and some compound sentences with *and*, *but*, *so*, or *or*.

1. _____

_____

2. _____

_____

3. _____

_____

4. _____

_____

5. _____

_____

6. _____

_____

STEP 3   **Check your work.**

Read your sentences. Use the writing checklist to look for mistakes, and use the editing symbols on page 168 to mark corrections.

Writing Checklist

❏ Does every sentence begin with a capital letter and end with a period?

❏ Does every sentence have a subject and a verb?

❏ Do the subjects and the verbs agree?

❏ Did you use some compound sentences?

❏ Did you use *and*, *but*, *so*, and *or* correctly in the compound sentences?

STEP 4   **Write a final copy.**

Correct your mistakes. Copy your final sentences in paragraph form and give the copy to your instructor.

UNIT FOUR

Memory

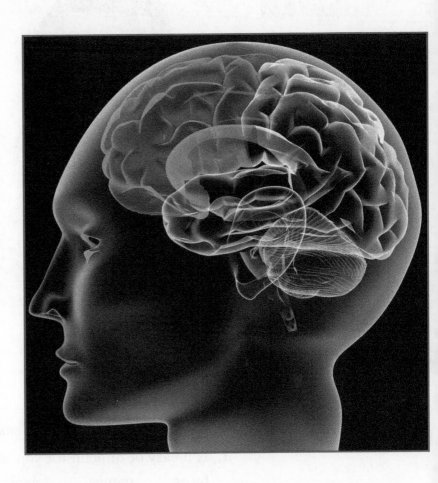

61

Memory Methods

PRE-READING

Discussion

Discuss the questions in pairs or small groups.

1. Is it easy or difficult for you to remember the following things?

   faces   names   telephone numbers   dates in history

2. Look at the picture and the title of the chapter. Can you guess what the chapter will be about? Check (✓) one of the answers.

   ____ how to find lost things

   ____ why we forget things

   ____ how to remember things

Vocabulary

A. *Read the boldfaced words and their definitions. Then complete each sentence with the correct word.*

> **instead:** in place of (someone or something)
> **memory:** the ability to remember things
> **method:** a way of doing something
> **order:** the way that you place things or put them on a list

1. These numbers are in _____: 7, 8, 9, 10.
2. After he hit his head, he lost his _____. He didn't even know who his wife was.
3. I don't want to go to the movies again. Why don't we go to a baseball game _____?
4. When you cook potatoes, which _____ do you use? Do you boil them or bake them?

B. *Read the boldfaced words and their definitions. Then complete each sentence with the correct word.*

> **imagine:** use your mind to think of new pictures, stories, ideas, etc.
> **memorize:** learn words, music, or facts so that you can remember them
> **practice:** a regular activity that you do to improve your skill at it
> **useful:** helpful for you to do or to get what you want

1. A dictionary is very _____ when you don't know the meaning of a word.
2. Close your eyes and _____ your bedroom. Do you see it in your mind?
3. I don't play tennis very often, so I'm not very good. I need more _____.
4. I have a vocabulary test tomorrow. I need to _____ the definitions of 50 new words.

Memory Methods

1   **Memory** is an important part of learning. It is also important in everyday life. With **practice**, most people can have an excellent memory. You just need to learn some simple **methods**.

2   The first method is *visualization*. When you visualize something, you make a picture of it in your mind. To help you remember, think of a really strange picture. Say, for example, you are in a large parking garage.[1] You park your car on level C in space[2] number five. You want to remember where you parked, so you close your eyes and **imagine** your car in that space on that level.[3] Will you remember that? Probably not. Now **instead**, imagine five cats inside the car. The cats are for level C. The five is for the number of the space. Because that picture is so strange, you will probably remember it.

3   The second method is **useful** when you need to remember a list of things in **order**. For example, imagine that you need to do a lot of things after work. They are all in different parts of town. You need to be at the dentist's office in an hour, so you don't have much time. You need to go to these places in this order: post office, supermarket, bank, and dentist's office. To remember, imagine the first letter of each place. Put the letters in the correct order. In this example, the letters are *p* (post office), *s* (supermarket), *b* (bank), and *d* (dentist). Then make a sentence with words that start with those letters, in that order. For example, your sentence might be: *Paul Smith buys dogs*. Then **memorize** it. Like the visualization method, this method works best if the sentence is a little strange.

4   There are more than just two memory methods. You can find others online. Go to a search engine[4] such as Google™, and do a search for "memory methods." Now, can you remember that parking garage from the beginning of the reading? Can you remember where the car is? The one with the five cats in it? And what about Paul Smith? Do you remember him? You see—memory methods really work. The next time you need to remember something, try one of them.

---

[1]**parking garage:** a large indoor area where you can leave your car
[2]**space:** an empty area in a parking garage that is big enough for one car
[3]**level:** a floor in a parking garage that has several floors
[4]**search engine:** a computer program that helps you find information on the Internet

Identifying Main Ideas

A. What is the main idea of the reading? Check (✓) the best answer.

_____ 1. With practice and good methods, most people can have a good memory.

_____ 2. It is very difficult for some people to improve their memories.

_____ 3. Visualization is the best way to remember things.

B. Underline the main-idea sentence of paragraph 2.

C. Underline the main-idea sentence of paragraph 3.

Identifying Details

Mark each statement T (true) or F (false).

_____ 1. It is easier to remember strange things than everyday things.

_____ 2. It is very difficult to have a good memory.

_____ 3. You should use the visualization method when you need to remember a list of things in order.

_____ 4. You can find more information about memory methods online.

READING SKILL

Understanding Pronoun Reference

Often writers do not want to repeat the same words, so they use pronouns. **Pronouns take the place of nouns or noun phrases.** A noun phrase is a noun and other words that describe the noun. When you are reading, it is very important to understand which words the pronouns replace.

EXAMPLES

- **Memory** is an important part of learning. **It** is also important in everyday life.

  (*The pronoun* **It** *replaces the noun* memory.)

- **The memory methods in the reading** are useful, and **they** are easy to learn.

  (*The pronoun* **they** *replaces the noun phrase* the memory methods in the reading.)

Practice

A. Read each sentence. Circle the word or phrase that the boldfaced pronoun replaces.

1. When you visualize (things), you make pictures of **them** in your mind. You see these things in your mind.

2. Because that picture is so strange, you will probably remember **it**.

3. For example, imagine that you need to do a lot of things after work. **They** are all in different parts of town.

4. Make a sentence with words that start with those letters. Then memorize **it**.

5. There are other memory methods. You can find **them** online.

6. And what about Paul Smith? Do you remember **him**?

7. You see—these memory methods really work. The next time you need to remember something, try one of **them**.

B. Read the paragraph. Write the words that the boldfaced pronouns replace.

The first thing I remember from my childhood is when I was three years old. I was with my sister. **(1) We** were sitting on a beach. I think that **(2) it** was in New Jersey. The sun was strong that day. **(3) It** was in my eyes. The sand was hot, and **(4) it** burned my feet. Our mother was trying to take a picture. **(5) She** told **(6) us** to smile, but **(7) we** started to cry. She took many pictures that day, but we were crying in all of **(8) them**.

1. _My sister and I_
2. _____
3. _____
4. _____
5. _____
6. _____
7. _____
8. _____

Reflecting on the Reading

Discuss the questions in pairs or small groups.

1. Which of these things are difficult for you to remember? Check (✓) your answers.

   ____ where you put your keys   ____ telephone numbers

   ____ important dates in history   ____ computer passwords

   ____ new words in English   ____ appointments

2. How do you remember the things in question 1 above? Explain your methods to a classmate.

Activating Your Vocabulary

Complete each sentence. Circle the letter of the best answer.

1. These words are in alphabetical _____: *green, guest, guy.*

   a. memory   b. order

2. I can _____ information for a test, but then I forget it as soon as the test is over.

   a. imagine   b. memorize

3. Close your eyes and _____ a beautiful place.

   a. imagine   b. memorize

4. If you want to play the piano well, you need a lot of _____.

   a. practice   b. order

5. I make vocabulary cards for any new words I learn. That's my _____ for learning vocabulary.

   a. memory   b. method

6. My father is very old, but his _____ is still very good.

   a. memory   b. practice

7. A good knife is _____ in the kitchen.

   a. method   b. useful

8. The blue dress was too small, so I bought the red one _____.

   a. in order   b. instead

Read the model paragraph.

MODEL

Summers were the best times in my childhood. I remember those summer days as always sunny. I never wanted them to end. My grandparents had a small house near the beach. I spent three months there with my mother, my grandmother, and my sister. My father and grandfather came on the weekends. They arrived on Friday night after dinner. My sister and I were so happy to see them! My father always brought us something special from the city. One time, he brought us new bicycles. We rode them everywhere. We felt like the luckiest girls in the world.

Using Pronouns

WRITING
SKILL

Writers use pronouns when they don't want to repeat a noun or noun phrase. When you use a pronoun, make sure you **use the correct form**.

The **subject pronouns** are *I, you, he, she, it, we,* and *they.* Subject pronouns come **before a verb**.

The **object pronouns** are *me, you, him, her, it, us,* and *them.* Object pronouns come **after a verb or a preposition**, for example *in, on, at, of,* or *to.*

EXAMPLE

OBJECT PRONOUN   SUBJECT PRONOUN

• My mother took pictures of **us. We** were crying in every picture.

When you use a pronoun, make sure it is **clear which word(s) the pronoun replaces**.

EXAMPLE

• **My mother** took **my sister's** picture. **She** was crying.

In this example, it is *not* clear which word the pronoun *She* replaces. Does it refer to "My mother" or to "my sister"? In this case, do not use a pronoun. Use the noun or noun phrase.

• My mother took my sister's picture. **My sister** was crying.

Practice

A. Read each sentence. Replace the repeated nouns with pronouns. Use the correct pronoun form (subject or object).

                                      He

1. My father wasn't at the beach. ~~My father~~ was working in the city. When my father came home, my mother showed my father the pictures. My father laughed.

2. The sand was very hot, and the sand burned our feet, so we put our feet in the water. The water was very cold. The water felt good.

3. I have good memories of the beach, but I don't have any good pictures of my sister and me there. My sister and I look unhappy in every photograph my mother took of my sister and me.

4. I still have those pictures. Those pictures are terrible, but those pictures make me smile. When I show those pictures to my son, my son laughs too.

B. Read each sentence. Is it clear which word the boldfaced pronoun replaces? Check (✔) if it is clear.

_____ 1. The beach was beautiful. **It** was in a small town.

_____ 2. The beach was in a small town in New Jersey. **It** was close to New York.

_____ 3. My grandparents had a house there. **It** wasn't a big house, but it was comfortable.

_____ 4. My grandmother, my mother, my sister, and I spent every summer there. My father and grandfather worked in the city. **He** visited us on the weekends.

_____ 5. Sometimes my mother came to the beach, and sometimes my grandmother came. When **she** came with us, she always made a big lunch.

_____ 6. My grandmother's lunches were the best, so we were happy when **she** came to the beach with us.

Editing

Read the paragraph. Correct the pronoun mistakes. There are six mistakes including the example.

At the end of the summer, I never wanted to go back to the city. One time, I decided to hide when it was time to leave. I waited until my mother and father were busy, so ~~My mother and father~~ *they* didn't notice me. I took my suitcase to my special hiding place. My special place was a very small house in the garden behind the big house. I was ready to live there for the winter. But my sister saw me, and my sister told my father. Then him came and got me. They wasn't angry with me, but I was angry with my sister. I didn't talk to them for a week.

WRITING ASSIGNMENT

Write a paragraph about your memory. Follow the steps.

STEP 1   Get ideas.

Work in pairs. Ask and answer the questions. If you don't know a word, check your dictionary or ask someone the meaning.

1. Do you have a good memory?
2. What kinds of things are easy for you to remember?
3. What kinds of things are difficult for you to remember?
4. When you need to remember something, what methods do you use? For example, how do you remember telephone numbers?
5. Would you like to improve your memory? Why or why not?

STEP 2   Write sentences.

Write sentences about your memory. Answer the questions above in order. Use pronouns to replace repeated words.

1. _____

   _____

2. _____

   _____

3. _____

_____

4. _____

_____

5. _____

_____

STEP 3 **Check your work.**

Read your sentences. Use the writing checklist to look for mistakes, and use the editing symbols on page 168 to mark corrections.

> ### Writing Checklist
> ❑ Does every sentence begin with a capital letter and end with a period?
> ❑ Does every sentence have a subject and a verb?
> ❑ Do the subjects and the verbs agree?
> ❑ Did you use the correct pronoun forms?

STEP 4 **Write a final copy.**

Correct your mistakes. Copy your sentences in paragraph form, and give the copy to your instructor.

Smell, Memory, and Sales

PRE-READING

Discussion

Discuss the questions in pairs or small groups.

1. Look at the chapter title and the picture. What do you think the reading will be about?
2. Can you remember a smell from your childhood? What is it? Why does it make you think of your childhood?

Vocabulary

A. Read the sentences. Match the boldfaced words with the definitions in the box.

_____ 1. You can buy the company's **products** in their stores or on their website.

_____ 2. Doctors and hospitals are trying to **develop** ways to help people with cancer.

_____ 3. The store isn't busy right now. There is only one **customer**.

_____ 4. There are so many things on the menu. It is really very difficult to **choose**.

> a. someone who buys things from a store or company
> b. design and produce something new
> c. decide which one of a number of people or things that you want
> d. things that people grow or make in order to sell them

B. Read the sentences. Match the boldfaced words with the definitions in the box.

_____ 1. Only **guests** can use the swimming pool for free.

_____ 2. Please **make sure** that you have two pencils. You will need them for the test.

_____ 3. You smell good! What kind of **perfume** are you wearing?

_____ 4. An **advertisement** in that magazine costs $100 a word. That's too expensive for our company.

> a. a liquid with a nice smell that women put on their skin
> b. people who are staying in a hotel
> c. a picture, a set of words, or a short movie intended to make people want to buy a product or use a service
> d. do something because it is important if you want a particular result

Smell, Memory, and Sales

1   Close your eyes. Think about a happy memory. What do you see? What do you smell? Do memories smell? Harald Vogt and Avery Gilbert think so. Smell and memory are very important to them. Why? They sell smells.

2   Who do they sell the smells to? And how can they sell a smell? Businesses come to Vogt and Gilbert for help. Vogt and Gilbert find a smell to go with the business's **product**. For example, Vogt and Gilbert worked with an expensive hotel in New York City. They **developed** a smell like expensive cologne[1] for the hotel's owners. Then they put it in the air of the hotel lobby.[2] Why did they **choose** the smell of cologne? A lot of businessmen stay at that hotel. The hotel's owners want their **guests** to feel like they are in an expensive men's club.[3] And rich men wear expensive cologne.

3   Using smell to sell things is not new. Bakers know that the smell of baking bread brings in **customers**. They always **make sure** that people on the street can smell the baking bread. Chocolate makers do the same thing. And of course, **perfume** makers sell smells.

4   In the past, only the food and perfume businesses used smell to sell their products. But today, more and more businesses are trying it, from hotels to airlines. Some companies put a special smell on the **advertisement** that they send to customers. For example, one car company uses a perfume on their brochures[4] that smells like a new car.

5   But do smells really sell? The answer seems to be yes. Smells become a part of our memories. And memory is important in sales. Why? When customers remember the name of a product, they usually choose it again. But there are a lot of choices these days, so it isn't easy to remember product names. That's why smell is important. It helps people remember.

6   In the future, will different computers and televisions have different smells? Vogt and Gilbert think so. They are sure that one day, most businesses will use smell to sell.

---

[1]**cologne:** a liquid with a pleasant smell that men put on their skin
[2]**lobby:** a large hall inside the entrance of a building
[3]**men's club:** To be a member of a club, you need to pay money to join. Businessmen often join clubs in order to meet other businessmen. At the club, they play golf or tennis, or have a drink and talk.
[4]**brochure:** a thin book that gives information or advertises something

Identifying Main Ideas

A. What is the main idea of the reading? Check (✔) the best answer.

_____ 1. Most people are good at remembering smells.

_____ 2. Today, more and more businesses are using smell to sell things.

_____ 3. Hotels use smell to make guests want to stay there.

B. Write the number of the paragraph next to its topic.

_____ 1. traditional uses of smell in sales

_____ 2. new uses of smell in sales

_____ 3. how Vogt and Gilbert sell smells

_____ 4. how memory and sales are related

Identifying Details

Complete each sentence. Circle the letter of the best answer.

1. Vogt and Gilbert _____.
   a. help businesses sell their products
   b. own a hotel

2. Vogt and Gilbert _____.
   a. develop smells to go with products
   b. sell perfume and cologne

3. In the past, smell was important in the _____.
   a. hotel and airline businesses
   b. food and perfume businesses

4. Today, some businesses are using smell to sell _____.
   a. televisions and computers
   b. cars

FROM READING TO WRITING

Reflecting on the Reading

Discuss the questions in pairs or small groups.

1. What are your favorite smells?
2. Do you have memories of any smells? What are they?
3. In the future, do you think that most products will have a smell?

Activating Your Vocabulary

Complete the sentences with the words from the box.

advertisement	customers	guests	perfume
choose	develop	make sure	products

1. We put an _____ in the Sunday newspaper because most people read the paper on Sundays.

2. Something smells like flowers. Are you wearing _____?

3. These rooms are not for _____. They are for the hotel managers.

4. She's one of the store's best _____. She spends thousands of dollars a year here.

5. Why did you _____ red? You look much better in blue.

6. That company makes school _____ such as pencils, pens, paper, and notebooks.

7. Please go back and _____ that you locked the door.

8. He is trying to _____ a product that will make old people look young.

WRITING

Read the model paragraph.

MODEL

> When I think of my childhood, I remember the smell of my mother's perfume. The name of the perfume was *Adore*. They don't make it now, but it was popular at that time. My mother only wore it when she went out at night. One time, I hid her perfume. I wanted her to stay at home. She didn't get angry with me. She just laughed. Today, she tells that story to everyone.

WRITING SKILL

Using Present Time and Past Time Together

When you write, you need to be clear about the time period that you are writing about. In English, we have **two ways to show time**. We use **verb tense** and **time expressions**. For example, an *-ed* on the end of a verb means that something happened in the past. The time expression *in the past* also tells you the time. Often, writers write about the past and the present in the same paragraph, or even in the same sentence.

To make the changes from one time to another clear, writers often use **time words and expressions**.

Some common **time words for the present** are *now*, *today*, and *still*.

Some common **time words for the past** are *in the past*, *at that time*, *one time*, and *ago*.

EXAMPLE

- ┌─ PAST ─┐   PAST
  In the past, only the food and perfume businesses **used** smell to sell
  ┌─ PRESENT ─┐   ┌─ PRESENT ─┐
  their products. **But today**, more and more businesses **are trying** it.

All main verbs have verb tense, but we do not use time expressions in every sentence. When we don't use a time expression, the **verb tense shows the time**.

EXAMPLE

          PRESENT   PRESENT
- A business **comes** to Vogt and Gilbert for help. They **find** a smell for
  the business's product. For example, Vogt and Gilbert **worked** with
  an expensive hotel in New York City.   └─ PAST ─┘

Practice

A. *Read the model paragraph again. Underline the time expressions.*

B. *Read the paragraph. Underline the time expressions. Circle the verb forms that are in the correct tense.*

Today most children (have)/ **had** their own bikes, but in the past

bicycles **are** / **were** expensive. Many families **don't have** / **didn't have**

the money for a bicycle. I was lucky. I **get** / **got** the first bicycle in my

(continued)

neighborhood. I **remember / remembered** when my father **bring / brought** it home. All of the kids in the neighborhood **are / were** there. Everyone **watch / watched** when I took my first ride. It **is / was** so exciting! Now I **have / had** a five-year-old son, and he still **ride / rides** that same bicycle.

Editing

Read the paragraph. Six of the underlined verbs (including the example) are in the wrong tense. Find the incorrect verbs and correct them.

When I <u>was</u> 19 years old, I *lived* ~~live~~ in Ecuador for a year. Many of my memories of Ecuador are of smells. I remember the day when I <u>smelled</u> and <u>taste</u> papaya for the first time. Papaya is a popular kind of fruit in Ecuador. It <u>has</u> a special smell. At breakfast on my first day in Ecuador, my host mother <u>give</u> me some strange orange fruit with a funny smell. At that moment, I <u>am</u> very homesick. I was trying not to cry. It <u>is</u> difficult to swallow that piece of papaya. That happened almost 30 years ago, but the smell of papaya still <u>made</u> me a little sad.

WRITING ASSIGNMENT

Write a paragraph about a smell that makes you remember a person, a place, or a time. Follow the steps.

STEP 1   Get ideas.

Work in pairs. Ask and answer the questions. If you don't know a word, check your dictionary or ask someone the meaning.

1. What smell do you remember?
2. Does it make you remember a person? A place? A time?
3. How old were you?
4. Where were you?
5. What happened?
6. How do you feel when you remember it?

STEP 2 **Write your paragraph.**

Complete the first sentence of the paragraph below. Then use information from your conversation with your partner to complete the rest of the paragraph.

When I smell _____, I remember _____

_____ .

_____

_____

_____

_____

_____

_____

_____

STEP 3 **Check your work.**

Read your paragraph. Use the writing checklist to look for mistakes, and use the editing symbols on page 168 to mark corrections.

Writing Checklist

❑ Does every sentence have a subject and a verb?

❑ Do the subjects and the verbs agree?

❑ Did you use the correct verb tense (present or past)?

❑ Did you use time words (present or past)?

❑ Did you use correct paragraph form?

STEP 4 **Write a final copy.**

Correct your mistakes. Copy your final paragraph and give it to your instructor.

Housing

Cohousing

Discussion

Discuss the questions in pairs or small groups.

1. Look at the picture. What do you see? Where are the people? What is happening?
2. The prefix *co-* means "together." Look at the picture and the title of the chapter. What do you think *cohousing* means?
3. What are some of the advantages (good things) of living together with a large group of people? What are some of the disadvantages (bad things)?

Vocabulary

A. Read the boldfaced words and their definitions. Then complete the paragraph with the correct words.

community:	a place such as a street or neighborhood and all of the people who live there
housing:	houses, apartments, etc. that people live in
residents:	people who live in a particular place
take care of:	keep something or someone in good condition

The cost of (1) _____ is very high in this part of the country. Most houses cost more than $300,000, and a one-bedroom apartment costs $1,000 a month. I'm lucky because I bought my house a long time ago when prices were low. I'm also lucky because I live in a wonderful (2) _____. I have good relationships with all of my neighbors. For example, my neighbors Tom and Betty (3) _____ my cat when I go on vacation, and I water their garden when they go away. I would not like to live in a place where the (4) _____ don't know each other. I like to know the people who live next to me.

B. Read the boldfaced words and their definitions. Then complete the paragraph with the correct words.

area:	a particular part of a place, city, country, building, etc.
follow:	do what someone tells you to do
own:	have something because you bought it or someone gave it to you
separate:	different

If you (1) _____ an apartment in this building, you can use the swimming pool, but you need to (2) _____ the rules. First, you cannot bring any food or drinks into the pool (3) _____. Second, there is a (4) _____ section of the pool that is only for residents who are 18 years and older. Children under the age of 18 cannot swim in that part of the pool.

Cohousing

1   Cohousing is a special kind of group housing. It began in Denmark many years ago. Today it is becoming popular all over the world. When people start a cohousing community, they are usually strangers. However, they have the same dream. They don't want to live alone. They want to live in a community. They want close relationships with their neighbors.

2   Both the individual and the group are important in cohousing communities. Individuals own and live in separate houses, but the community owns all of the land. The houses are very close together. There aren't any fences[1] between them. In front of the houses, there is usually a large open area. Everyone in the community can use that area. Children can play there. Other residents can walk or ride their bikes there.

3   The common house is the center of the cohousing community. The common house is a house that all of the residents own together. Most common houses have a large dining room and kitchen. Residents cook and eat together there once or twice a week. There are also play areas for children and recreation[2] areas for adults, a guest room, and a laundry room.

4   The residents of the cohousing community are like one big family. They take care of the common land. They often eat together. When a resident has a problem, the neighbors help. They drive a sick neighbor to the doctor, or take care of a neighbor's children. And in most cohousing communities, there are people of all ages, from the very young to the very elderly.

5   Most residents of cohousing are very happy. They love the community life. However, cohousing is not a good choice for everyone. Residents of cohousing communities make decisions together. For example, they meet and decide how to take care of the common areas. They also decide how often they will eat together. Then everyone agrees to follow the group's decision. If you don't like to make decisions in a group, you will probably not be happy in a cohousing community. Also, if you like to spend a lot of time alone, cohousing is probably not a good choice for you.

----

[1] **fence:** a structure made of wood, metal, etc. that surrounds a piece of land and keeps people or animals in or out
[2] **recreation:** an activity that you do for fun

Identifying Main Ideas

A. What is the main idea of the reading? Check (✔) the best answer.

_____ 1. People who live in cohousing are happy.

_____ 2. When people start a cohousing community, they are usually strangers.

_____ 3. Cohousing is a special kind of group housing.

B. Where could you add the sentences? Write 2 for paragraph 2, 3 for paragraph 3, and so on.

_____ 1. Residents with cars give rides to neighbors who don't drive.

_____ 2. The residents have group meetings there.

_____ 3. Individual residents do not own the land.

Identifying Details

What do people who live in a cohousing community share? Check (✔) the correct answers.

_____ 1. land

_____ 2. cars

_____ 3. pets

_____ 4. meals

_____ 5. doctors

_____ 6. the common house

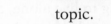

Identifying Topic Sentences

A topic sentence gives the main idea of a paragraph. The topic sentence is usually the first sentence of the paragraph. **The topic sentence introduces the topic of the paragraph and the main idea.** The main idea gives the writer's opinion, feeling, or idea about the topic.

EXAMPLE

┌──────TOPIC──────┐ ┌──────────MAIN IDEA──────────┐
• **The common house** is the center of the housing community.

Practice

Read each paragraph. Circle the letter of the best topic sentence.

1. _____. When you live alone, you can eat whatever you want at any time. You can listen to music or watch TV at any time of day or night, and you don't need to worry about bothering anyone. You don't need to take care of anyone. You are free. That is why I like to live alone.

   a. Many people live alone.

   b. Living alone is great.

   c. It is not easy to live alone.

2. _____. In the city, you can find everything you need. You can eat out at a different restaurant every night. You can see all of the new movies. You can go shopping at the best stores. If you live in the city, you will never be bored. There is always something interesting to do.

   a. Cities have wonderful restaurants.

   b. Cities are the best places to live.

   c. A lot of people live in cities.

3. _____. I am young and single, and most of my neighbors are too. It is easy to make friends. There is a lot of nightlife, so I'm never bored. There are also many inexpensive cafés and restaurants in the area, so I don't need to cook. I eat almost every meal out. I love everything about my neighborhood.

   a. It is great to be young and single.

   b. If you move to my city, you should look for an apartment in my neighborhood.

   c. My neighborhood is perfect for me.

4. _____. I'm going to live alone, and I don't need a lot of space. I don't like to cook, so I don't need a large kitchen. I don't have much furniture, and I don't want to buy any more. I don't want to spend a lot of money. That's why I think a small apartment is best for me.

   a. I would like to find a small, simple apartment.

   b. Small apartments are comfortable.

   c. Large apartments cost a lot of money.

Reflecting on the Reading

Discuss the questions in pairs or small groups.

1. Do you have anything similar to cohousing in your country? Explain.

2. Which of the following people would probably be happy in cohousing? Explain your answers.

- a 5-year-old only child
- an 18-year old college student
- a 25-year-old single woman
- a 50-year-old single man
- a young couple with two small children
- a 75-year-old widow (a woman whose husband died)

3. Would you like to live in cohousing? Why or why not?

Activating Your Vocabulary

Complete each sentence. Circle the letter of the best answer.

1. When you own a house, you don't need to _____.
   a. pay rent
   b. take care of it

2. If you and your sister have separate bedrooms, there are at least _____ in your house.
   a. two bedrooms
   b. three bedrooms

3. You need to follow the rules, or you can't _____.
   a. agree with us
   b. play with us

4. Take care of your little brother. This is a _____ area.
   a. dangerous
   b. safe

5. We need to find housing. We are looking for _____.
   a. a resident
   b. an apartment

6. In my community, there are two beautiful _____.
   a. cities
   b. parks

7. He doesn't _____ here. He is not a resident.
   a. live
   b. work

8. You can walk your dog in this area of the _____.
   a. park
   b. rule

Read the model paragraph.

MODEL

> I come from Boston, Massachusetts. In Boston, there are many different kinds of housing. There are a lot of three-family houses, with one apartment on each floor. In most apartments in three-family houses, there are two bedrooms, a living room, a kitchen, and one bathroom. There isn't usually a dining room, but there is an eating area in the kitchen. There are also a lot of apartment buildings in Boston. There are some single-family homes in Boston, too, but not very many. The single-family houses in Boston are usually quite large, with three or four bedrooms. Usually, only the richest residents live in single-family homes. Most people in Boston live in apartment buildings or three-family houses.

WRITING SKILL

Using *There is / There are*

When we write about **places**, we often use *There is* or *There are* to introduce information about the place. In sentences that begin with *There is / There are*, the **subject comes after the verb**. *There* is NOT the subject.

There	is (not)	a/an	singular subject
There	is	an	open area.
There	isn't	a	swimming pool.

There	are (not + any)		plural subject
There	are		people of all ages.
There	aren't any		fences.

Practice

Complete each sentence with is, are, isn't, or aren't.

1. In the common house of our cohousing community, there _____is_____ a large dining room, but there _____ any guest rooms.

2. There _____ a large play area for the children, and there _____ two swimming pools.

3. There _____ a large laundry room in the common
   house, so there _____ any washing machines in the
   individual houses. Individuals don't need to have their own
   washing machines.

4. There _____ two parking spaces for each household.
   There _____ also a small parking area for guests.

5. There _____ any tennis courts, but there
   _____ a health club with exercise machines.

Replacing *There is* / *There are* with Pronouns

We often use *There is* or *There are* when we **introduce a topic for the
first time**. After we introduce the topic with *There is* or *There are*, we
use **subject or object pronouns** (for example *it*, *they*, or *them*) to refer
to the topic.

EXAMPLES

┌─── NEW TOPIC = COMMON HOUSE ───┐ ┌─── (SUBJECT) COMMON HOUSE ───┐
- There is **a common house**. **It** is the center of the community.

┌─── (OBJECT) COMMON HOUSE ───┐
Everyone in the community owns **it**.

┌─── NEW TOPIC = GROUP MEALS ───┐ ┌─── (SUBJECT) GROUP MEALS ───┐
- There are **group meals** twice a week. **They** are in the common house.

┌─── (OBJECT) GROUP MEALS ───┐
We enjoy **them** very much.

Practice

***Read the paragraph. Complete each sentence with* there, it, they, *or*
them.**

(1) _____There_____ is a new cohousing community in my town.

(2) _____It_____ is a small community with only ten houses.
Nine of the houses are sold, but (3) _____ is one left.
My wife and I looked at (4) _____ last weekend.
(5) _____ is small but very nice. (6) _____ are
27 residents in the other nine houses. We met (7) _____
last weekend. (8) _____ welcomed us and made us feel
very comfortable.

Write a paragraph about your neighborhood or about housing in your country. Follow the steps.

STEP 1   **Get ideas.**

Work in pairs. Choose a topic for your paragraph. Ask and answer the questions. If you do not know a word, check your dictionary or ask someone the meaning.

❏ **Topic 1:** Your neighborhood

1. Where do you live now?
2. Describe your neighborhood. For example, are there a lot of stores? Are there any restaurants? Is there a park?
3. Describe your neighbors. For example, are there a lot of children in the neighborhood? Are there a lot of students? Do you know your neighbors' names?
4. Do you like your neighborhood? Why or why not?

❏ **Topic 2:** Housing in your country

1. What city and country are you from?
2. What kinds of housing are there in your city? For example, are there a lot of single-family homes? Are there a lot of large apartment buildings?
3. Describe a typical home in your country. For example, how many rooms are there? What kinds of rooms are there? Is there a dining room? Is there a laundry room? Is there a separate room for guests? Is there an outdoor area, for example a garden or a yard?
4. If you are living in a foreign country, how is a typical home in your country different from a typical home in the country you are in?

STEP 2   **Write your paragraph.**

Complete one of the paragraphs below by writing about your topic. Use information from your conversation with your partner. Use some sentences with *There is / There are.*

❏ **Topic 1**

I live _____. In my neighborhood, there

_____

_____

My neighbors _____

_____

_____

I like/don't like my neighborhood because _____

_____

_____

❏ **Topic 2**

In my city, there are different kinds of housing. There are _____

_____

_____

_____

Many people in my city live in _____

_____

_____

_____

STEP 3 **Check your work.**

Read your paragraph. Use the writing checklist to look for mistakes, and use the editing symbols on page 168 to mark corrections.

> ### Writing Checklist
> ❏ Does every sentence begin with a capital letter and end with a period?
> ❏ Does every sentence include a subject and a verb?
> ❏ Do the subjects and verbs agree?
> ❏ Did you use *There is / There are* to introduce your topics?
> ❏ Did you use subject and object pronouns correctly?

STEP 4 **Write a final copy.**

Correct your mistakes. Copy your final paragraph and give it to your instructor.

The Micro-Compact Home

PRE-READING

Discussion

Discuss the questions in pairs or small groups.

1. Look at the picture of the micro-compact home. *Micro* means "small" and *compact* means "small compared with other things of the same type or kind." Does this home look comfortable to you? Why or why not?

2. Check (✓) the things that you think a micro-compact home has.

   ____ a kitchen   ____ a place to sit down

   ____ a table   ____ a bed

   ____ a bathroom   ____ a television

Vocabulary

A. Circle the letter of the word or phrase that is closest in meaning to the boldfaced word.

1. This house is very big. There is **space** for all of my furniture.

    a. housing   (b.) room   c. variety

2. The house is not **complete**. There isn't any glass in the windows, and there aren't any doors.

    a. big   b. finished   c. special

3. The **size** of the house is perfect for a large family. There are five large bedrooms.

    a. how big or small something is   b. how typical something is   c. the form of something

4. I love the **design** of the house. It is simple but beautiful at the same time.

    a. place or location   b. how something looks and is made   c. special rules

B. Circle the letter of the word or phrase that is closest in meaning to the boldfaced word.

1. The use of space in this office is very **efficient**. There is a place for everything. You don't need to spend time looking for things.

    a. well organized   b. attractive   c. uncomfortable

2. It is difficult to move around in this room. There are too many chairs and tables. It is **crowded**.

    a. acceptable to live in   b. full of things or people   c. difficult to understand

3. We used a lot of expensive **materials** in the house. We used the best wood, beautiful stone, and special glass for the windows.

    a. products you can make things from   b. gifts for family and friends   c. special characteristics

The Micro-Compact Home

1   Look around your house or apartment. How big is it? How much of that **space** do you really use? All of it? Half of it? Less than half? How much space do you really need to be comfortable? Is 70 square feet (6.5 square meters) enough? The makers of the micro compact home, or *m-ch*, think it is.

2   The m-ch is a very small but **complete** home for one or two people. It is only 70 square feet in **size**. In that small space, there is a kitchen, a bathroom with a shower, and a living area with a flat-screen television. There is heat and air-conditioning.

3   How is there enough space for all of this in just 70 square feet? The answer is careful **design** and **efficient** use of space. To make the m-ch, builders got ideas from the design of old Japanese tea houses. They also took ideas from cars, boats, and airplanes. In the living area, there are two fold-up beds.[1] There is a large table below the beds. The table slides[2] into a small space in the wall. At different times of the day, the same area can be a living room, a dining room, or a bedroom.

4   Why is the m-ch so small? There are two reasons. First, the m-ch is for people who need a place to live for a short time and don't need a lot of space. For example, the m-ch is perfect for college students, business people, and people on vacation. Second, the makers of the m-ch wanted it to be beautiful but not too expensive. Builders use the best **materials** to make it beautiful. But the m-ch is small, so they don't need a lot of these materials, and it doesn't cost a lot to make.

5   As the world becomes more **crowded** and housing becomes more expensive, many people think that small houses like the m-ch will become more popular. But is the m-ch really comfortable? Yes, say a group of students who are living in them. In an experiment[3] at a university in Germany, six students agreed to live in a community of micro-houses for just one semester. However, they were so comfortable in their small houses that they asked to stay for the rest of the year. And now other students at the university want their own micro-compact homes.

---

[1] **fold-up bed:** a bed that you can bend in the middle so that it can fit in a small space when you aren't using it
[2] **slide:** move quietly and smoothly
[3] **experiment:** a scientific test that you do to learn about something

Identifying Main Ideas

Read each question. Circle the letter of the best answer.

1. What is the main idea of the reading?
   a. The micro-compact home is small but comfortable and complete.
   b. The micro-compact home is popular with college students.
   c. The micro-compact home is attractive, but it is expensive.

2. What is the main idea of paragraph 2?
   a. The m-ch is small but complete.
   b. The m-ch has heat and air-conditioning.
   c. The m-ch is just one room.

3. What is the main idea of paragraph 3?
   a. The design of the m-ch is like a Japanese tea house.
   b. The design of the m-ch is very efficient.
   c. The design of the m-ch is like the design of a car or airplane.

4. What is the main idea of paragraph 4?
   a. The m-ch is small because it is for college students.
   b. The m-ch is small for two reasons.
   c. The m-ch is small, so it is good for short stays.

5. What is the main idea of paragraph 5?
   a. The m-ch is an experiment.
   b. The m-ch is very popular today with college students.
   c. The m-ch will probably become more popular in the future.

Identifying Details

Answer the questions. Write complete sentences.

1. How many people can live in one m-ch?

   _____

2. How big is the m-ch?

   _____

3. What is inside the m-ch?

   _____

(continued)

4. Where did the builders get their ideas for the design of the m-ch?

   _____

5. Who did the builders make the m-ch for?

   _____

FROM READING TO WRITING

Reflecting on the Reading

Discuss the questions in pairs or groups.

1. How big is the place you live in now? Do you use all of the space in your place? Explain your answer.
2. Do you think that the m-ch is attractive? Why or why not?
3. Would you like to live in the m-ch? Why or why not?

Activating Your Vocabulary

Complete the sentences with the words from the box.

complete	design	materials	space
crowded	efficient	size	

1. We can't move into the house yet. It isn't _____. The kitchen and bathrooms are not finished.
2. Builders need a lot of _____ when they build a house. They need wood, nails, glass, and bricks, among other things.
3. This room is too _____. I think we should put the sofa in another room.
4. Do you have any extra _____ in your garage? I need a place to put my bike during the winter.
5. I like this rug, but I don't think it's the right _____. It's too small for this big room.
6. I don't like the _____ of that car. It isn't attractive, and it's very uncomfortable to drive.
7. This kitchen is big, but it is not very _____. The stove is too far away from the sink, the refrigerator is too small, and there is no place to put the dishes.

Read the model paragraph.

MODEL

> The m-ch is the perfect home for a student. It has everything that a student needs. There is a large table where you can study. When you're tired of studying, you can lie down on the comfortable bed and watch the flat-screen television. If you're hungry, you can go into the modern kitchen and make a snack. But the best thing about the m-ch is the size. It is small and easy to clean. It takes me only 15 minutes to clean the m-ch. That means I have more time to study and have fun with my friends.

WRITING
SKILL

Using Descriptive Adjectives

We use adjectives to describe nouns. Adjectives often come **in front of the nouns** they describe.

EXAMPLE

                  ADJECTIVE   NOUN

• The answer is **careful design**.

Adjectives also come **after linking verbs** such as *be, feel,* and *become.*

EXAMPLES

NOUN	LINKING VERB	ADJECTIVE
• The **m-ch**	is	**perfect** for college students.
		(describes the noun m-ch)
• The **students**	felt	**comfortable** in the m-ch.
		(describes the noun students)
• The **world**	is becoming	**crowded**.
		(describes the noun world)

Notice that there is **only one form** for adjectives. We use the same form to describe singular and plural nouns.

Practice

Read each sentence. Underline the adjectives. Circle the nouns or pronouns that the adjectives describe.

1. How <u>big</u> is (it)?

2. The m-ch is very small but complete.

3. In that small space, there is a kitchen, a bathroom with a shower, and a comfortable area with a large television.

4. There is a large table below the beds.

5. At different times of the day the same area can be a living room, a dining room, or a bedroom.

6. The makers of the m-ch wanted it to be beautiful but not too expensive.

7. Small houses like the m-ch will become popular in the future.

8. But is the m-ch really comfortable?

9. A group of German students lived in micro-houses for a year.

10. The students found them to be very comfortable.

Editing

Read the paragraph. Correct the use of there is, there are, *and descriptive adjectives. There are seven mistakes including the examples.*

                   comfortable city   *It*

Boston is a ~~city comfortable~~ to live in. ~~There~~ is the perfect size. It are not very big, so you can walk from one area of the city to another. It is also a city pretty. There is a lot of big trees, beautiful parks, and old buildings. They are also wonderfuls libraries and museums.

Write a paragraph about a place. Follow the steps.

STEP 1   **Get ideas.**

Work in pairs. Choose a topic for your paragraph. Then ask and answer the questions. If you don't know a word, check your dictionary or ask someone the meaning.

❏ **Topic 1:** The best place to study

❏ **Topic 2:** The best place to fall in love

❏ **Topic 3:** The best place to live

1. Where is the place?
2. What does it look like? Describe it.
3. Why is it a good place to study/fall in love/live? What does it have?
4. What is the best thing about the place?

STEP 2   **Write your paragraph.**

Complete the paragraph below by writing about your topic. Use information from your conversation with your partner. Use adjectives to describe the place, and use some sentences with *There is / There are*.

_____ is the best place to _____

_____

_____

_____

_____

_____

_____

_____

_____

_____

STEP 3   Check your work.

Read your paragraph. Use the writing checklist to look for mistakes, and use the editing symbols on page 168 to mark corrections.

Writing Checklist

❑ Does every sentence begin with a capital letter and end with a period?

❑ Do the subjects and verbs in every sentence agree?

❑ Did you use *There is / There are* to introduce your topics?

❑ Did you use subject and object pronouns correctly?

❑ Did you use adjectives correctly?

STEP 4   Write a final copy.

Correct your mistakes. Copy your final paragraph and give it to your instructor.

UNIT SIX

The Art
of Medicine

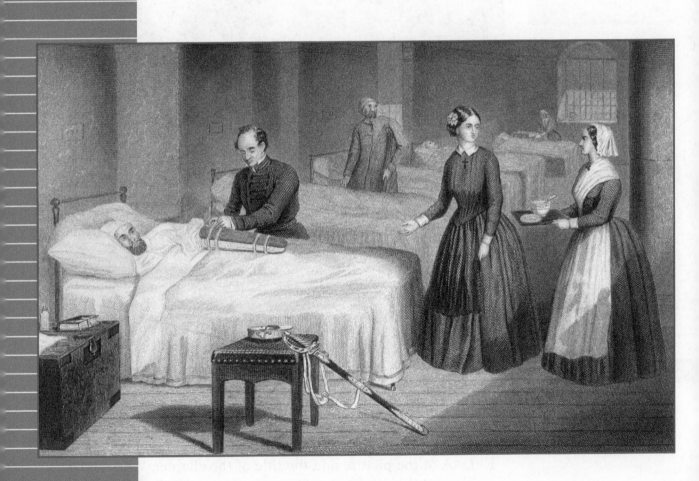

One Doctor, One Patient, Two Different Worlds

**In this chapter
you will:**

• read a true story
about a doctor
and a patient

• learn to identify
time order when
you read

• write
a paragraph
using
time clauses
with *before,*
when, and *after*

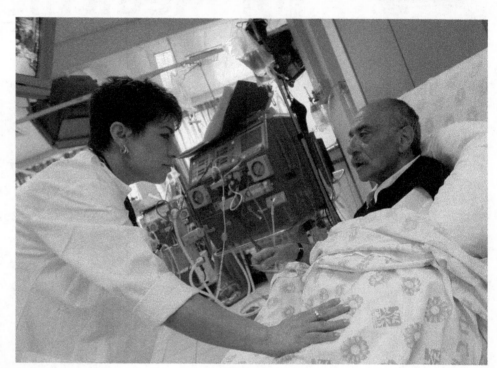

PRE-READING

Discussion

Discuss the questions in pairs or small groups.

1. Look at the picture and the title of the chapter. Who are the
people? What is happening in the picture? What do you think
the reading will be about?
2. In your culture, when someone is dying, does the doctor tell
the person the truth? Does the doctor tell the family the truth?
3. Do you think it is important for you and your doctor to come
from the same culture? Why or why not?

Vocabulary

A. Read the sentences. Match the boldfaced words with the definitions in the box.

_____ 1. There are many **patients** in the hospital. The doctors and nurses take care of them.

_____ 2. Nobody knows why the man is sick. The doctors are trying to **find out** what is wrong with him. They still don't know.

_____ 3. The best **treatment** for a cold is to drink a lot of water and stay in bed.

_____ 4. She was in a car accident and broke her leg badly. She had an **operation** to fix it.

> a. learn new information as a result of tests or experience
> b. the process of cutting into someone's body to repair or remove a part that is damaged
> c. people who are getting medical help from a doctor or hospital
> d. a way of making a sick or injured person better

B. Read the sentences. Match the boldfaced words with the definitions in the box.

_____ 1. My parents don't practice the same **religion**. My father is Jewish. My mother is Catholic.

_____ 2. My grandmother is still very sick. Her doctor will not **allow** her to leave the hospital.

_____ 3. I am sick, but I **refuse** to call the doctor or go to the hospital. I can take care of myself.

_____ 4. He looks healthy, but **actually** he is very sick.

> a. in fact (saying something is true of a situation, rather than what people may think)
> b. say that someone can do something
> c. say that you will not do something
> d. a special set of beliefs in one or more gods and the activities related to this belief

One Doctor, One Patient, Two Different Worlds

1   Can you die from a cultural difference? That is the question that a filmmaker wanted to explore. So she made a movie about the true story of a doctor, his **patient**, and their two very different cultures.

2   The doctor in the movie is an American. The patient in the movie is from Afghanistan. In 1988, this Afghan man came to the United States with his wife and ten children. In 2000, he started to feel sick. When he went to the hospital, the doctors found a serious problem. He had stomach cancer. He needed an **operation**. After he had the operation, he felt much better. So when his doctor told him he needed more **treatment**, he said no. But did he understand his American doctor? Did his doctor understand him? Was the patient's life in danger because he and his doctor were from different cultures? That is what the filmmaker wanted to **find out**.

3   **Religion** was one difference between the patient and the doctor in the movie. The patient **refused** the treatment for religious reasons. However, according to the movie, the doctor didn't ask him why his religion did not **allow** it. That was a big mistake. **Actually**, the patient's religion does allow the treatment. The problem was how the doctor planned to give him the medicine, through a needle[1] in his arm. There were other ways to give the medicine, for example in a pill.[2] But the doctor never told him that. Why not? The doctor thought that the medicine was the problem.

4   Another difference was language. The patient did not speak English, but his daughters did. The doctor thought that the daughters told their father everything. But they didn't. They never told him he had cancer. In the movie, a family friend explained that in Afghan culture the doctor does not speak to the patient directly. He speaks to the family. And often the family does not tell the patient the truth. So did this patient know that he was dying? It is not clear in the movie.

5   The Afghan man died from cancer before the movie was finished. The filmmaker makes it very clear in the movie that the doctor gave the patient excellent medical care. She also makes it clear that the doctor respected and cared about his patient very much. But was the patient's life shorter because he and his doctor came from different cultures? We will never know. That is why the filmmaker made the movie. She wants both patients and doctors to think about how important culture might be in medical treatment.

---

[1] **needle:** a thin sharp hollow piece of metal that puts medicine or drugs into your body
[2] **pill:** a small hard piece of medicine that you eat/swallow

Identifying Main Ideas

A. What is the main idea of the reading? Complete the sentence.

The Afghan man's story can help both _____ and
_____ understand the importance of culture.

B. What is the main idea of each paragraph? Complete the sentences.

1. (paragraph 2)

   The _____ and the _____ came from
   different cultures. Perhaps they did not really understand each
   other.

2. (paragraph 3)

   A very important difference between the patient and his doctor
   was _____.

3. (paragraph 4)

   The patient and his doctor did not _____ the same
   _____.

Identifying Details

Complete the summary of the reading with the words from the box.

Afghanistan	cultures	different	mistakes
American	dies	languages	

In this movie about a true story, a man from (1) _____
and his (2) _____ doctor have an extremely difficult time
understanding each other. The patient and his doctor come from
different (3) _____ and speak different (4) _____.
The patient, his family, and his doctor make a lot of (5) _____
because they don't understand each other's cultures or languages. The
doctor does his best, but in the end the patient (6) _____.
We will never know if his life was shorter because he and his doctor
came from (7) _____ cultures.

**READING
SKILL**

Understanding Time Order

When you read a story, it is important to understand the order of the actions or events. Writers often use **time clauses to show time order**. A time clause is a group of words that shows the relationship between two different actions or events in a sentence. Time clauses begin with **time words** such as *when*, *after*, or *before*.

Time clauses with *when* show that the action happened at the same time, or just a little bit before, the action in the main clause.

EXAMPLE

TIME WORD

├─────── TIME CLAUSE ───────┤ ├──────── MAIN CLAUSE ────────┤
- **When** he went to the hospital, the doctors found a serious problem.

   (He went to the hospital. At that time, the doctors found a serious problem.)

Time clauses with *after* show that the action happened before the action in the main clause.

EXAMPLE

┌── TIME CLAUSE: 1ST ACTION ──┐ ┌─ MAIN CLAUSE: 2ND ACTION ─┐
- **After** he had the operation, he felt much better.

   (First, he had the operation. Then he felt much better.)

Time clauses with *before* show that the action happened after the action in the main clause.

EXAMPLE

┌── TIME CLAUSE: 2ND ACTION ──┐ ┌─ MAIN CLAUSE: 1ST ACTION ─┐
- **Before** he went to the hospital, he called his daughters.

   (First, he called his daughters. Then he went to the hospital.)

Practice

A. *Read each sentence. Circle the time word. Then underline the main clause once and the time clause twice.*

1. The man's daughters were with him (when) he went to the hospital.

2. He did not feel well (before) he had the operation.

3. The patient was an important man in Afghanistan before he came to the United States.

4. After the man and his family left Afghanistan, they moved to the United States.

5. When he died, his family was very sad.

B. Read each sentence in Exercise A again. Write a 1 under the first action that happened and a 2 under the second action. If both actions happened at the same time, write a 1 under both clauses.

1. <u>The man's daughters were with him</u> <u>when he went to the hospital.</u>
              1   1

2. <u>He did not feel well</u> <u>before he had the operation.</u>
       1   2

FROM READING TO WRITING

Reflecting on the Reading

Discuss the questions in pairs or small groups.

1. Do you think that the doctor did anything wrong? Explain your answer.
2. Do you think that the patient's family did anything wrong? Explain your answer.
3. What do you think that doctors will learn when they watch this movie? What will patients learn?

Activating Your Vocabulary

Complete each sentence. Circle the letter of the best answer.

1. His doctor allowed him to leave the hospital, so he _____.
   a. stayed   b. went home

2. Treatments are for _____.
   a. patients   b. religions

3. My religion is very important to me. Actually, religion is _____ in my life.
   a. the most important thing   b. not very important

4. How did you find out the patient's name? Did one of the nurses _____ you?
   a. tell   b. prevent

(continued)

5. When he hurt his leg, he refused to go to the doctor. I was _____.

   a. happy   b. worried

6. It was a serious operation. She was in the _____ for weeks.

   a. hotel   b. hospital

7. She is not my patient. She goes to another _____.

   a. customer   b. doctor

8. In my religion, we believe that there is only one _____.

   a. God   b. patient

WRITING

Read the model paragraph.

MODEL

> When I was two years old, my grandparents' dog bit me. It was a Saturday night. My sister was four years old, and she was playing with the dog. I was on the floor. Suddenly my sister pulled its tail and ran out of the room. When the dog turned around, it saw me. Then it bit me. I started to scream. When my mother saw the blood, she started to scream, too. My parents put me in the car and drove me to the hospital. My sister stayed at home with my grandparents. Fortunately, it wasn't a serious bite, but my mother was angry at my sister for a long time. After that happened, they never allowed us to play with the dog again.

WRITING
SKILL

Using Time Clauses

Both the main clause and the time clause have a subject and a verb. When the **time clause begins the sentence**, put a **comma (,)** between the time clause and the main clause.

EXAMPLE

```
┌──────── TIME CLAUSE ────────┐  COMMA  ┌──── MAIN CLAUSE ────┐
```
• **After** he had the operation, he felt much better.

When the **main clause begins the sentence**, do NOT put a comma (,) between the time clause and the main clause.

EXAMPLE

```
  ┌────── MAIN CLAUSE ──────┐ ┌────────── TIME CLAUSE ──────────┐
```
- He felt much better **after** he had the operation.

Practice

Combine each pair of sentences to make one new sentence with a time clause and a main clause. Add a comma where necessary.

1. The man was in his 50s. He left Afghanistan.

   When *the man was in his 50s, he left Afghanistan.*

2. He got sick. He and his family had a good life.

   Before _____

3. His daughters went with him. He visited the doctor.

   _____ when _____

4. The doctor told his patient about the treatment. The patient refused.

   When _____

5. The filmmaker finished the movie. The patient died.

   _____ after _____

Editing

Read the paragraph. Correct the mistakes by adding commas, periods, or capital letters. There are six mistakes including the example.

When I was five years old ⌃ my mother became very sick She was giving my sister and me a bath. Suddenly, she started to scream. when my father heard her, he ran into the room She was on the floor. He picked her up and carried her out of the bathroom. My sister and I were very scared. after he left the room we didn't speak or move. We just sat there. A few minutes later, my father came back. He carried us into our bedroom. Before he left the room he kissed us goodnight. We heard an ambulance a few minutes after he left the room. We didn't see our mother again for six weeks.

Write a paragraph about an experience with a hospital, a doctor, or a dentist. Follow the steps.

STEP 1 **Get ideas.**

Work in pairs. Choose a topic for your paragraph. Then ask and answer the questions. If you don't know a word, check your dictionary or ask someone the meaning.

❑ **Topic 1:** A time when you or a family member needed to go to the hospital

❑ **Topic 2:** An experience at the doctor or dentist's office (the experience can be real or imaginary)

1. How old were you?
2. Where were you?
3. Who was there?
4. What happened?
5. How did you feel?
6. How did the story end?

STEP 2 **Write your paragraph.**

Complete the paragraph below by writing about your topic. Use information from your conversation with your partner. Use some time clauses with *when, after,* and *before.*

When I was _____ years old, _____

_____

_____

_____

_____

_____

_____

_____

_____

_____

STEP 3   Check your work.

Read your paragraph. Use the writing checklist to look for mistakes, and use the editing symbols on page 168 to mark corrections.

Writing Checklist

❑ Did you use past tense correctly?

❑ Did you use time clauses correctly?

❑ Did you include a subject and a verb in both the main clause and the time clause?

❑ Did you use commas where necessary?

STEP 4   Write a final copy.

Correct your mistakes. Copy your final paragraph and give it to your instructor.

An Artist and a Doctor

Dr. Chuang and one of his paintings

PRE-READING

Discussion

Discuss the questions in pairs or small groups.

1. Dr. Chuang has two jobs: artist and doctor. Do you know anyone who has two jobs? What are the two jobs?
2. Do you think it is strange for a doctor to also be an artist? Why or why not?
3. Do you know any artists? Are they full-time artists, or do they have another job?

Vocabulary

A. Read the boldfaced words and their definitions. Then complete each sentence with the correct word or phrase.

> **a while:** a period of time, especially a short one
>
> **graduate:** get a diploma or degree by completing your studies at a school, college, or university (past: *graduated*)
>
> **heal:** get better or make someone get better after an injury or sickness
>
> **project:** some work that you plan carefully and that often takes a long time

1. He cut his hand with a knife. It is a serious cut. It will take a long time to _____.

2. She didn't finish the _____ on time, so she lost her job.

3. They are going to _____ from high school next year. Then they'll go to college.

4. We talked for _____ before we went to bed.

B. Read the boldfaced words and their definitions. Then complete each sentence with the correct word.

> **creative:** good at thinking of new ideas or making new things
>
> **nature:** the world and everything in it that people have not made, such as plants, animals, or the weather
>
> **nervous:** worried or scared
>
> **sensitive:** a sensitive person is able to understand the feelings, problems, etc., of others

1. I love _____. I like to be outside. I need to live in a place with trees and fresh air.

2. My son is very _____. If he sees an animal that is hurt, he starts to cry.

3. My daughter is _____. She paints and draws all the time. I think she is going to be an artist.

4. I hate going to the dentist. I always get _____ before I go there.

An Artist and a Doctor

1   Chen-Chieh Chuang believes that medicine is an art. He also believes that art is good medicine. Chuang is an artist, but he is also a doctor. Chuang believes that both art and medicine help people to **heal**. Before he sees his first patient every morning, Chuang paints. ". . . Art heals me," he says. And he hopes to use his art to heal others.

2   Chuang was born in Taiwan. He learned to paint when he was a child. From a very young age, he wanted to be both an artist and a doctor. When he went to college, he studied art and biochemistry[1] at Brown University in Rhode Island. After Chuang **graduated** from Brown, he taught art in New York City for a year. Then he began medical school at Yale University.

3   After medical school, Chuang worked as a doctor in poor communities. He traveled and worked all over the United States, from Arizona to Alaska. During this time, he also continued painting. He painted the beautiful things of **nature**, for example plants, flowers, and birds.

4   A few years ago, Chuang decided to work in one place for **a while**. He opened a medical office in Massachusetts. He also began to show and sell his paintings, and he started a class for medical students called Art and Medicine. Chuang designed it to help students see the relationship between art and medicine. He wants to help students become **sensitive** and **creative** doctors.

5   In 2005, Chuang bought his own building and moved his medical practice[2] there. "It's my big art **project**," says Chuang. Outside the building, there are thousands of flowers and trees. In the waiting area, there are large windows and plants everywhere. Chuang's paintings and photographs are on the walls. There are also books on art, religion, sports, and of course, medicine.

6   Next to the waiting area, there is a kitchen. There is always fruit there for the patients. Sometimes Chuang bakes bread, and the smell fills the waiting area. Chuang says, "Most of the time when people come to the doctor's, they are already **nervous**. I want to make them feel comfortable."

7   Patients love everything about Dr. Chuang's medical practice, from the gardens outside to the beautiful paintings inside. But they especially love Dr. Chuang, the artist and doctor who created this special place.

----

[1]**biochemistry:** the science of the chemistry of living things
[2]**medical practice:** a doctor's office and the work he or she does there

Identifying Main Ideas

What is the main idea of the reading? Complete the sentence.

Dr. Chuang believes that both art and medicine help people to

_____.

Identifying Details

Complete the time line of Dr. Chuang's life with information from the reading.

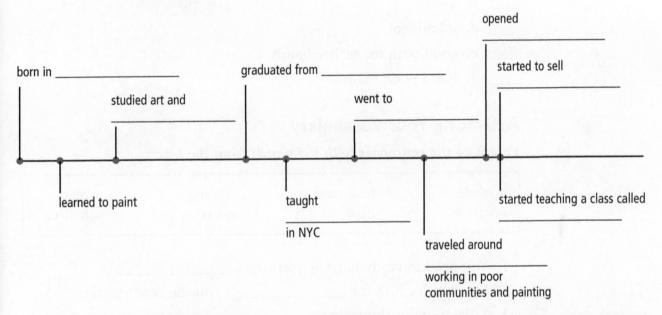

born in _____

studied art and
_____

learned to paint

graduated from _____

went to

taught
_____
in NYC

traveled around
_____
working in poor
communities and painting

opened
_____

started to sell
_____

started teaching a class called
_____

Cheng-Chieh Chuang,
Butterfly and Lily

Reflecting on the Reading

Which characteristics below are necessary for a good artist? Which ones are necessary for a good doctor? Mark each characteristic A (artist) or D (doctor). Explain your answers.

_____ a. creative

_____ b. sensitive

_____ c. kind

_____ d. intelligent

_____ e. good with his or her hands

_____ f. has a good memory

Activating Your Vocabulary

Complete the sentences with the words from the box.

a while	graduate	nature	project
creative	heal	nervous	sensitive

1. You need to study hard or you won't _____.

2. I waited for him for _____, but he never came.

3. I like to paint things from _____, such as mountains, trees, plants, and animals. I don't like to paint cities.

4. I don't have to tell her when I'm not feeling well. She knows immediately. She is very _____.

5. He is so _____. He can always find the answer to a problem even when everyone else thinks that there is no answer.

6. I am working on a _____ on giraffes for a class. I have to visit the zoo and watch the giraffes, and then I have to write about them.

7. I am showing my paintings for the first time at an art show next week. I'm excited but also a little bit _____.

8. I cut my hand a week ago, but it won't _____. I think I need to go and see a doctor.

Read the model paragraph.

MODEL

Dr. Atul Gawande is both an excellent doctor and a famous writer. He was born on November 5, 1965 in Brooklyn, New York. His parents are from India. Dr. Gawande started writing when he was in medical school. At first, he wrote short articles for magazines. In his articles, he wrote about the difficult decisions doctors make every day. He also wrote honestly about doctors' mistakes. People loved his articles, and in 2002 he wrote his first book, *Complications: A Surgeon's Notes on an Imperfect Science*. It became popular right away. In 2006, Dr. Gawande received a very special award for his creative work in medicine and literature, the MacArthur award. In 2007, he finished his second book, *Better: A Surgeon's Notes on Performance*. Today Dr. Gawande lives, writes, and practices medicine in the Boston area.

WRITING SKILL

Using Prepositional Phrases of Time

A prepositional phrase includes a preposition (for example *in*, *on*, or *at*) followed by a noun. We use **prepositional phrases of time** to say **when something happened**. The preposition we use depends on the noun. Here are some common preposition of time and noun combinations.

in + year or month	*at* + point in time	*for* + time period	*on* + day
in 2000 in May	at 7:00 at the end of the week	for a while for a week	on Thursday on Christmas

Prepositional phrases of time usually come at the **beginning or end** of the sentence.

EXAMPLES

PREPOSITIONAL PHRASE

- **In 2005** Chuang started his own medical practice.

PREPOSITIONAL PHRASE

- Chuang started his own medical practice **in 2005**.

Practice

Complete each sentence with the correct preposition.

1. _____*For*_____ several years Chuang traveled around the United States.

2. He decided to stay in one place _____ a while.

3. _____ 6:00 A.M. Chuang usually starts painting.

4. He opened Lakeside Family Practice _____ 2005.

5. _____ September he started teaching a course in art and medicine.

6. He shows his paintings at art shows _____ Saturdays and Sundays.

Editing

Read the paragraph. Correct period, comma, and preposition mistakes. There are six mistakes including the examples.

My father is a wonderful singer. He learned to sing when he was a
little boy. ~~In~~ *On* Sundays he sang at church. He joined a singing group,
when he was in high school. At the age of 15, he went to New York City
with his group. They were there in one week. Every day they took
classes with the best music teachers in the city. They sang at Carnegie
Hall in the end of the week. He says that he will remember that trip on
the rest of his life.

WRITING ASSIGNMENT

Write a paragraph about the life of a person you find particularly interesting. Follow the steps.

STEP 1   Get ideas.

Work in pairs. Ask and answer the questions. If you don't know a word, check your dictionary or ask someone the meaning.

1. What is the person's name?
2. When and where was the person born?

3. What is interesting about this person's life? What did he or she do? How is this person special?
4. Is this person alive today? If so, what is this person doing now? If not, how and when did this person die?

STEP 2   **Write your paragraph.**

Write a paragraph about the person you chose. Use information from your conversation with your partner. Use prepositional phrases of time and time clauses.

_____

_____

_____

_____

_____

_____

_____

_____

_____

STEP 3   **Check your work.**

Read your paragraph. Use the writing checklist to look for mistakes, and use the editing symbols on page 168 to mark corrections.

> **Writing Checklist**
> ❏ Is the order of events clear in your paragraph?
> ❏ Did you use verb tenses (present, past, future) correctly?
> ❏ Did you use prepositions of time correctly?
> ❏ Did you use time clauses correctly?
> ❏ Did you use commas correctly?

STEP 4   **Write a final copy.**

Correct your mistakes. Copy your final paragraph and give it to your instructor.

The Working World

Doing Business in the United Kingdom

PRE-READING

Discussion

Discuss the questions in pairs or small groups.

1. Look at the picture. What city do you think it is taken in?
2. What countries does the United Kingdom include?
3. Which statements are true about business people in the United Kingdom? Check (✓) your answers. If you are not sure, guess.

   _____ Men and women wear suits.

   _____ There is a lot of respect for age and experience.

   _____ Business people make decisions quickly.

   _____ Business people do not show their feelings.

Vocabulary

A. *Read the boldfaced words and their definitions. Then complete the paragraph with the correct words.*

> **expect:** think that something will happen
> **negative:** something bad about an idea, plan, etc.
> **patient:** able to deal with a problem or wait for something without getting angry or upset
> **proud:** feeling happy because you think that you, someone in your family, your country, etc. has done something good

When you visit another country, don't (1) _____ to understand everything right away. It takes a long time to feel comfortable in a new culture. You need to be (2) _____. And remember that most people are (3) _____ of their culture. They do not like it when people from other countries say (4) _____ things about their country. Always try to find something nice to say.

B. *Read the boldfaced words and their definitions. Then complete the paragraph with the correct words.*

> **in charge:** in the position of organizing or controlling something
> **neutral:** not causing people to disagree and express strong opinions and feelings
> **reserved:** not liking to show your feelings or talk about your thoughts and problems
> **voices:** the sounds people make when they speak or sing

When you are doing business in a foreign country, you need to watch and listen carefully. First, listen to how people speak. Are their (1) _____ soft or loud? Second, watch how people behave. Do they show their feelings on their faces, or are they (2) _____? Who is (3) _____ of the group? How does that person behave? How does that person show that he or she is the leader? Finally, when you are not talking about business, talk about (4) _____ topics, such as the weather or sports. Never discuss politics or religion.

Doing Business in the United Kingdom

1   If you want to do business in an English-speaking country, you should learn English, of course. But that is just the first step. You also need to understand the culture. However, there are large cultural differences among English-speaking countries. The differences between the United Kingdom (UK) and countries with shorter histories are especially large. Australia and the United States, for example, are much younger than the UK. Their business cultures are also different. Here is some information that can help you if you do business in the UK.

2   First of all, remember that the UK includes four countries: England, Wales, Scotland, and Northern Ireland. Each country is **proud** of its history. Do not make the mistake of calling everyone "English." Instead, use the correct term, "British."

3   Second, when you plan a business trip to the UK, choose your team carefully. The British have more respect for age and experience than people in most other English-speaking countries. Always include older, more experienced people on your team. Do not put a young team member **in charge**, even if he or she is the most senior member[1] of the group.

4   Third, dress formally,[2] in a dark suit. Do not wear stripes.[3] In the UK, stripes on clothing such as ties can mean that the wearer is a member of a special group. It is best to wear clothing of just one color, such as black, gray, or dark blue. Do not wear bright colors such as pink or yellow.

5   Fourth, keep small talk[4] safe and **neutral**. For example, talk about the weather or your trip. Most British people are **reserved**, so do not ask personal questions. And do not **expect** your British colleagues[5] to show their feelings on their faces or in their **voices**. Speak more softly than you might in the United States.

6   Fifth, don't try to sell yourself. Sell your business. Your British colleagues are more interested in your business than in you. They do not expect or want gifts or friendship from business colleagues. They do not usually want to know about your family or how you spend your free time. Do not spend a lot of time on small talk. Talk about business.

----

[1]**senior member:** the person who has the most years of experience and is often older than the others in the group
[2]**formally:** in a traditional way, not in a relaxed way
[3]**stripe:** a long narrow line of color
[4]**small talk:** polite friendly conversation about everyday things that are not very important
[5]**colleagues:** people who work with you in the same office or organization

7   Finally, be **patient**. Business decisions often take time in the United Kingdom. Older companies find change especially difficult. Do not try to get your British colleagues to make a fast decision. Most of the time, a fast decision will be **negative**.

8   In conclusion, remember that the UK has a long history and many traditions. In business, the cultural rules are not the same as they are in younger countries such as Australia and the United States.

Identifying Main Ideas

A. **What is the main idea of the reading? Underline the main idea sentence in the first paragraph.**

B. **Underline the topic sentences of paragraphs 2, 3, 4, 5, and 6.**

C. **Where could you add the sentences? Write 2 for paragraph 2, 3 for paragraph 3, and so on.**

___4___ 1. Never wear jeans.

_____ 2. Find out which countries of the United Kingdom your British colleagues come from.

_____ 3. Never expect a decision at a business meeting.

_____ 4. Sports are usually a safe topic.

_____ 5. Be very polite to people who are older than you.

_____ 6. Don't talk about your personal opinions or interests.

Identifying Details

Answer the questions with information from the reading.

1. Why shouldn't you call people from the UK "English"?
   The UK includes _____, _____, _____, and _____.

2. Why should you include older, more experienced people on your team?
   The British have _____ for age and experience.

3. What colors should you wear?
   Wear just one color, such as _____.

(continued)

4. What shouldn't you talk about?

The British do not usually want to talk about _____.

5. Why do you need to be patient?

_____ often take time in the United Kingdom. A fast decision will be negative.

Understanding Signal Words

Writers use certain words to signal, or show, the relationships among their ideas. These words are called **signal words**. Signal words help you understand the **organization** of a reading. You learned some of the words that signal time changes, for example *in the past*, *still*, *today*, and *in the future*.

This chapter's reading explains a **process**. A process tells the reader how to do something. The signal words for a process are often **numbers**, such as *first of all*, *second*, and *third*, or words that tell the **order of the steps** in a process, for example *then*, *after that*, and *finally*. Process signal words usually come at the beginning of the sentence.

EXAMPLE

- **First of all,** choose your team carefully. Remember that the British have respect for age and experience. **Second,** pack appropriate clothing. Business people in the UK usually dress formally, in dark suits. **Third,** don't try to sell yourself. Sell your business. Your British colleagues are more interested in your business than in you.

Practice

A. *Look at the reading again and circle the process signal words. Discuss your answers with a classmate.*

B. *Number the sentences from the reading in the order that they appear in the text.*

____ **1.** Put an older person in charge of your team.

____ **2.** Don't wear stripes or bright colors.

____ **3.** Don't expect a fast decision.

____ **4.** Talk about neutral topics.

____ **5.** Talk about your project or product, not about yourself.

_1_ **6.** Use the term *British*, not *English*.

Reflecting on the Reading

Discuss the questions in pairs or small groups.

1. Look at the list of actions. Are they acceptable for business people to do in the UK? Are they acceptable in your country?
   - move their hands a lot when they speak
   - wear sneakers (athletic shoes) to work
   - shake hands with women and men
   - tell colleagues about their family

2. In what ways are business people from your country similar to business people from the UK? In what ways are they different?

Activating Your Vocabulary

Complete each sentence. Circle the letter of the best answer.

1. The person who is in charge is _____.
   a. the boss   **b.** a co-worker

2. Parents are usually proud of their children when the _____ do something well.
   a. parents   **b.** children

3. If you expect someone to do something, you think that the person _____ do it.
   a. will   **b.** won't

4. A reserved person doesn't _____ in front of other people.
   a. cry   **b.** smile

5. You can hurt your voice if you _____ a lot.
   a. eat   **b.** scream

6. I don't have _____ about that. I'm neutral.
   a. a decision   **b.** an opinion

7. Respect other people's cultures. _____ negative things about their customs and traditions.
   a. Don't say   **b.** Say

8. Don't _____. I'm not very patient.
   a. take a long time   **b.** worry

Read the model paragraph.

MODEL

> If you want to do business in the United States, here are a few rules that will help you. First of all, always shake hands with both male and female colleagues. Women and men expect to be treated the same in American culture, especially in business. Second, do not be too formal. In general, Americans are less formal in business than people from many other cultures. For example, if an American colleague tells you to use his or her first name, do it. Finally, if an American colleague invites you out for lunch or dinner, accept the invitation. If you don't, your colleague might think that you are rude.

WRITING SKILL

Using the Imperative

Writers often use the **imperative** form of the verb when they are **explaining a process** or **giving advice**. There is usually no subject with the imperative form, but everyone understands that the subject is *You* (the reader or readers). There is only one form of the imperative for both singular and plural *you*.

EXAMPLES

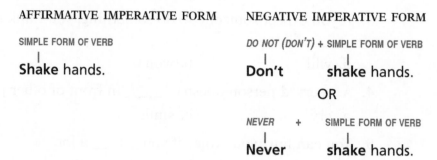

AFFIRMATIVE IMPERATIVE FORM

SIMPLE FORM OF VERB

Shake hands.

NEGATIVE IMPERATIVE FORM

DO NOT (DON'T) + SIMPLE FORM OF VERB

Don't **shake** hands.

OR

NEVER + SIMPLE FORM OF VERB

Never **shake** hands.

Practice

A. *Work in pairs. Read the model paragraph again. Circle the imperative verb forms.*

B. *Imagine that you are giving advice to a new teacher. Change each sentence to the imperative form.*

  1. A good teacher is patient.

    Be patient.

2. A good teacher doesn't get angry at students.

Don't get angry at students.

3. A good teacher listens to students.

_____

4. Good teachers prepare lessons carefully.

_____

5. Good teachers never scream at students.

_____

6. Good teachers make lessons interesting.

_____

7. Good teachers don't forget students' names.

_____

8. A good teacher is creative.

_____

WRITING ASSIGNMENT

Write a paragraph that gives advice. Follow the steps.

Step 1 **Get ideas.**

Choose a topic and complete the chart. Then explain your chart to a partner. Give examples if necessary. If you don't know a word, check your dictionary or ask someone the meaning.

❑ **Topic 1:** Advice to a foreigner who wants to do business in your country

❑ **Topic 2:** Advice to a foreigner who wants to study in your country

DO	REASON	DON'T DO	REASON
1.		1.	
2.		2.	
3.		3.	

STEP 2 Write your paragraph.

Use the cues to complete the paragraph about your topic. Use some affirmative and some negative imperative verb forms.

If you want to _____ in _____, here are a
                   (STUDY OR DO BUSINESS)   (YOUR COUNTRY)

few rules that will help you. First, _____
                                        (WRITE THE FIRST RULE)

_____.

_____.
(GIVE AN EXAMPLE OR EXPLAIN WHY THE FIRST RULE IS IMPORTANT IN YOUR CULTURE)

Second, _____.
              (WRITE THE SECOND RULE)

_____.
(GIVE AN EXAMPLE OR EXPLAIN WHY THE SECOND RULE IS IMPORTANT IN YOUR CULTURE)

Finally, _____.
              (WRITE THE THIRD RULE)

_____.
(GIVE AN EXAMPLE OR EXPLAIN WHY THE THIRD RULE IS IMPORTANT IN YOUR CULTURE)

STEP 3 Check your work.

Read your paragraph. Use the writing checklist to look for mistakes, and use the editing symbols on page 168 to mark corrections.

Writing Checklist

❏ Does every sentence begin with a capital letter and end with a period?

❏ Did you use the correct affirmative forms of the imperative?

❏ Did you use the correct negative forms of the imperative?

STEP 4 Write a final copy.

Correct your mistakes. Copy your final paragraph and give it to your instructor.

E-Mail: Terrific Tool or Time-Waster?

PRE-READING

Discussion

Discuss the questions in pairs or small groups.

1. Do you use e-mail? If so, do you use it for work, for your personal life, or for both?
2. If you don't use e-mail, why don't you use it?
3. What are the advantages of using e-mail? What are the disadvantages?

Vocabulary

A. *Read the definitions. Then read the first paragraph of the reading on the next page. Write the base form of each boldfaced word from paragraph 1 next to its definition.*

BOLDFACED WORD	DEFINITION
1. ____depend on____	: be affected by something that is not fixed and could change
2. _____	: use something in a way that is not effective
3. _____	: something that you use to do a particular job or to achieve something
4. _____	: share information, ideas, or opinions with someone

B. *Read the definitions. Then look for the boldfaced words with the same definitions in paragraphs 2–6 of the reading. Write the paragraph number and base form of each boldfaced word next to its definition.*

PARAGRAPH	BOLDFACED WORD	DEFINITION
1. __3__	____limit____ :	stop an amount or number from getting bigger than a particular amount
2. ____	_____ :	a piece of information that you leave for someone instead of speaking to him or her
3. ____	_____ :	involve someone or be important to someone
4. ____	_____ :	make a process or activity stop for a short time

E-Mail: Terrific Tool or Time-Waster?

1   E-mail helps workers to **communicate** at any time, from any place. But does e-mail make our work lives easier? Does it make us better workers? The answer **depends on** how we use it. E-mail can be an important **tool**, but it can also be a way to **waste** time. How can workers make sure that e-mail is a tool and not a time-waster? Here are some simple steps to follow. They can help you use e-mail more efficiently at work.

2   First of all, turn off the sound in your computer that tells you that you have a new e-mail **message**. That "You've got mail!" sound is like a telephone or a doorbell. It **interrupts** your work. When you hear it, you will want to check your messages. And it will take you at least a few minutes to get back to work after that. Multiply[1] that by the number of e-mail messages you get a day. Do you see how much time you waste because of that little sound?

3   Second, **limit** how often you check your e-mail. Try checking it only three times a day, for example, at 9:00, 12:00, and 4:00. Also, limit the time you spend reading and answering e-mail each time. Fifteen minutes is usually long enough.

4   Third, use a separate e-mail account[2] for work and personal life. Do not give your work address to friends or family, and do not give your personal address to people at work. If you are working on several projects at one time, use a separate e-mail account for each one. That way, if one project is very important, you can check the e-mail for that account only.

5   Fourth, ask everyone to write a very specific subject line[3] when they send you an e-mail message. If they do this, you won't have to read all new messages every time you open your e-mail. You can look quickly at the subject lines and then decide which messages you should answer right away. You can read the others later.

6   Finally, do not use "reply to all"[4] when you answer e-mail. Only send the message to the person or people who need to read your answer. That way, you won't fill your colleagues' inboxes[5] with information that they don't need. And they won't waste time reading messages that do not **concern** them.

7   If you follow these simple steps, you will be a more efficient worker. Best of all, you will be able to leave the office earlier.

---

[1] **multiply:** make a number bigger by adding the same number to it several times
[2] **e-mail account:** an electronic mailbox
[3] **subject line:** a word or phrase at the top of an e-mail message that briefly tells the reader what the e-mail is about
[4] **reply to all:** send an e-mail answer to everyone that received the message that you are answering
[5] **inbox:** the place in your e-mail account where you can find new messages

Identifying Main Ideas

A. Who is this article written for? Check (✔) the correct answers. (There is more than one correct answer.)

_____ 1. parents who communicate with their children by e-mail

_____ 2. businesses where workers communicate by e-mail

_____ 3. teenagers who communicate with their friends by e-mail

_____ 4. people who use e-mail at work

B. Complete the sentence. Check (✔) the best answer.

The writer thinks that _____.

_____ 1. people waste a lot of time at work because of e-mail

_____ 2. e-mail is the best way for workers to communicate with each other

_____ 3. companies should not allow their workers to use e-mail

Identifying Details

Check (✔) the statements that are true according to the reading.

_____ 1. The "You've got mail!" sound in your computer is useful.

_____ 2. It is not efficient to check your e-mail every time you get a new message.

_____ 3. You should check your e-mail at the same time every day.

_____ 4. Most workers should have at least two e-mail accounts.

_____ 5. You should answer all of your e-mail messages right away.

Reflecting on the Reading

Work in small groups. Ask and answer questions to complete the survey about e-mail use. Then report to the class on your group's use of e-mail.

WHO . . .	NUMBER OF STUDENTS
never uses e-mail but would like to?	
never uses e-mail and doesn't want to?	
uses e-mail for work or school?	
uses e-mail to communicate with family and friends?	
has more than one e-mail account?	
wastes a lot of time on e-mail?	
saves a lot of time by using e-mail?	

Activating your Vocabulary

Complete the sentences with the words from the box.

communicate	depends on	limit	tool
concern	interrupt	message	waste

1. He isn't here right now. Would you like to leave a _____?
2. Don't look up every new word in your dictionary. You should _____ yourself to five words a page.
3. Get to work. Don't _____ any more time.
4. Never _____ the teacher when he's speaking. Wait for him to finish.
5. The telephone is an important _____ for communication.
6. I'm not sure where we're going to live. It _____ where we can find jobs.
7. You are a good worker, but you need to learn to _____ better with your co-workers. You are often impatient with them.
8. I am not going to talk to you about my personal life. It doesn't _____ you.

Read the model paragraph.

MODEL

Do you want to become more efficient at work? Here are some simple steps you can follow. First of all, plan your workday around your energy levels. Work on creative projects at times of the day when you feel very awake and have a lot of energy. Save work that is not very creative for those times of the day when you feel tired and your energy level is low. Second, keep your desk neat. Make a special place for everything that you use at work. After you use something, return it to its place. That way you won't waste time looking for things. Finally, if there is something that you do every day, do it at the same time every day. It will become a habit, and you won't waste time trying to remember what you have to do.

WRITING
SKILL

Using Signal Words

Writers use **signal words** to show the **relationships between their main ideas**. The signal words that you choose depend on the relationship you are trying to show. We often put a signal word at the **beginning** of a sentence, with a **comma** after it. Here are some common signal words and the relationships they are used to show.

SIGNAL WORDS	RELATIONSHIP BETWEEN YOUR MAIN IDEAS
First of all, *Second,* *Third,* *Fourth,* *Finally,*	• You want to **make several main points** about one topic. • The order of the points is not important. • For example, you want to give someone advice on how to become more efficient at work.
First, *Second,* *Next,* *Then,* *After that,* *Finally,*	• You want to **explain how to do something** that has several steps. • The order of the steps is important. • For example, you want to teach someone how to use a machine.

Practice

These sentences explain how to open an e-mail account with the search engine Google. Number the sentences in the correct order.

____ 1. After you fill in the basic information, choose a user name and a password.

____ 2. If you completed everything correctly, a message on the screen will tell you that you were successful.

____ 3. You will see a form asking you for basic information such as your name and address.

_1_ 4. First, go to the home page for the search engine Google at www.google.com, find the link called *Gmail*, and click on it.

____ 5. If you are going to use this e-mail account for work, choose a user name that sounds professional. For example, use your name followed by the year you were born.

____ 6. After you type in your user name, choose a password that is easy for you to remember, but that no one else knows. Never use your birthday or your street address. Type in your password two times.

_2_ 7. Next, click on *Set up a new account*.

____ 8. Finally, go back to www.google.com and click on *Sign up for Gmail*. Type in your user name and password, and start using your new e-mail account.

Editing

Add the signal words in parentheses to the paragraphs. Change capital letters to lowercase letters and add commas wherever necessary.

1. (*first, then, after that, next, finally*)

Using an automatic teller machine (ATM) can be confusing.

Here are the basic steps. ^(First, put) ~~Put~~ your card in the machine. Enter

your password. Read the choices on the screen, for example, *get*

cash or *make a deposit*. Choose what you want to do by pressing the

number next to the action that you want, follow the instructions

on the screen. Don't forget to take your card when you finish.

(continued)

2. (*first of all, second, finally*)

Is it difficult for you to manage your money? Here is some advice that can help you. Do not spend money that you don't have. If you want to buy something, save the money and pay in cash. Never use credit cards. Don't eat your money. That is, do not go out to restaurants, and do not eat take-out food. Cook and eat at home. Pay all of your bills immediately. That way, the money will not be in your account and you can't spend it. Remember, money that you owe is not your money.

WRITING ASSIGNMENT

Write a paragraph that explains how to do something. Follow the steps.

STEP 1   Get ideas.

Work in pairs. Choose a topic. Ask and answer the questions. If you don't know a word, check your dictionary or ask someone the meaning.

❑ **Topic 1:** How to be a better student

1. What kinds of things do good students do? (Be specific.)
2. Why do they do those things?
3. What kinds of things don't good students do? (Be specific.)
4. Why don't they do those things?

❑ **Topic 2:** How to use a cell phone

1. What is the first step? What vocabulary do you need to explain the step?
2. What is the second step? What vocabulary do you need to explain this step?
3. What are the next steps? What vocabulary do you need to explain these steps?
4. What is the final step? What vocabulary do you need to explain it?

STEP 2 **Write your paragraph.**

Use one of the topic sentences below and information from your conversation with your partner to write a paragraph. Use signal words wherever necessary.

❑ **Topic 1:** You can do several things to become a better student.

❑ **Topic 2:** Using a cell phone for the first time can be confusing. Here are some simple steps that you should follow.

STEP 3 **Check your work.**

Read your paragraph. Use the writing checklist to look for mistakes, and use the editing symbols on page 168 to mark corrections.

Writing Checklist

❑ Did you use the imperative correctly?
❑ Did you use signal words?
❑ Did you explain each of the main points or steps?
❑ Did you use correct paragraph form?

STEP 4 **Write a final copy.**

Correct your mistakes. Copy your final paragraph and give it to your instructor.

What's Next?

Is 50 the New 30 and 70 the New 50?

Jane Fonda

Robert Redford

PRE-READING

Discussion

Discuss the questions in pairs or small groups.

1. Who are the people in the photographs? How old do you think they are?
2. Look at the title of the chapter and the pictures. What do you think the numbers mean? What do you think the reading will be about?

Vocabulary

A. Read the definitions. Then read the first two paragraphs of the reading on the next page. Write the base form of each boldfaced word from paragraphs 1 and 2 next to its definition.

BOLDFACED WORD   DEFINITION

1. _____ : able to move and do things easily

2. _____ : usual; the amount that you get by adding several numbers together and then dividing the total by the number of numbers you added together

3. _____ : person with special skills or knowledge of a subject

4. _____ : stop working at the end of your working life

B. Read the boldfaced words and their definitions. Then complete each sentence with the correct word.

client:	someone who pays to use the services of a business, a lawyer, etc.
healthy:	good for your body or mind
improve:	become better, or make something better
population:	the number of people who live in a place

1. Smoking is not _____. It is very bad for you.

2. The _____ of the United States is about 300,000,000.

3. You need to _____ your grades. If you don't, you will not graduate this year.

4. He is an important _____. He gives us a lot of business. Make sure that he is comfortable.

Is 50 the New 30 and 70 the New 50?

1   People in the United States are living longer. The **average** American will live to be 78. One hundred years ago this number was 48. By the year 2030, about 20 percent of Americans will be over the age of 65. Some **experts** say that Americans are living longer because they are taking better care of themselves. Many 50-year-olds today look and act like 30-year-olds. And many 70-year-olds feel like they are 50.

2   Dr. Hal Hockfield is a family doctor. Many of his patients are over 50. He says, "People are working longer, and thinking younger . . . they're not **retiring** early. . . . There are people 75 and 80 who are still working, keeping their bodies and minds **active**."

3   Joanne Sgro is a personal trainer.[1] She has about ten **clients** age 50 and older. They play tennis, dance, and ride horses. "Exercise and **healthy** living is part of their lives. They are well-educated and well-off[2] . . . so they have the time and interest to take care of themselves. . . . [They] think exercise is fun . . ." she says.

4   Older Americans are also keeping their minds active. Many colleges and universities allow seniors[3] to take classes. For example, at Boston University, people 58 and older can take classes with college students. These students are often the same age as their grandchildren. The cost? Just $75. The same classes cost their younger classmates $2,000 or more. Many seniors want to take classes, so they retire near universities.

5   Because the American **population** is getting older, ideas about beauty are changing, too. In the past, people didn't think of older actors as beautiful. For that reason, many female actors in Hollywood stopped working when they were 30. But today, celebrities[4] such as Jane Fonda (72), Christie Brinkley (55), and Madonna (51), are still popular. And actors such as Robert Redford (73) and Tom Hanks (53) continue to star in[5] movies. As Tom Hanks said, ". . . at 50, I feel like 34. . . . And at 60, I'll feel like 30, so actually, I'm getting younger."

6   Of course, most Americans are not as lucky as Tom Hanks. About 10 percent of American seniors are poor. Many have serious health problems. But for older Americans with money and good health, life is **improving** all the time.

---

[1] **personal trainer:** someone who teaches people how to exercise and stay healthy
[2] **well-off:** rich
[3] **senior:** person who is 60 years old or older
[4] **celebrity:** a famous person
[5] **star in:** be the main character in a movie, TV program, etc.

Identifying Main Ideas

A. *What is the main idea of the reading? Check (✔) the best answer.*

_____ 1. There are more older Americans than ever before.

_____ 2. The American population is getting older but feels younger.

_____ 3. The United States is changing a lot these days.

B. *Which sentences are main-idea sentences, and which are supporting sentences? Write M (main idea) or S (supporting sentence).*

_____ 1. Americans' ideas of beauty are changing as the population gets older.

_____ 2. American seniors are staying mentally active.

_____ 3. Many universities allow seniors to take classes.

_____ 4. Many seniors go to personal trainers.

_____ 5. Jane Fonda and Robert Redford continue to star in Hollywood movies.

_____ 6. American seniors are staying physically active.

Identifying Details

Complete the sentences with the numbers from the box. Be careful. There are three extra numbers.

10	20	30	50	70	75	78	80	100

1. They say that _____ years ago, the average American died at age 48.

2. Today, the average American lives to age _____.

3. Americans today are living about _____ years longer than they did 100 years ago.

4. In 2030, _____ percent of the American population will be older than 65.

5. If you are 58 years old or older, you can take a course at Boston University for $_____.

6. About _____ percent of American seniors are poor.

Understanding Cause and Effect

When you read about *why* something happened or exists, it is important to understand the **cause** and its **effect or result**. Writers often use words like ***because*** and ***so*** to make causes and results clear for the reader. When you read, pay attention to words that explain *why*.

EXAMPLES

┌──────────── CAUSE (WHY) ────────────┐   ┌──────── RESULT ────────┐
* Many seniors want to take classes, **so** they retire near universities.

┌──────── RESULT ────────┐   ┌──────── CAUSE (WHY) ────────┐
* Americans are living longer **because** they take care of themselves.

Practice

A. Look at the reading. Underline the sentences with because **and** so.

B. Match the causes and results from the reading.

CAUSE

_____ 1. Americans are taking better care of themselves.

_____ 2. Older Americans want to take college classes.

_____ 3. The American population is getting older.

_____ 4. Many older Americans are well-educated and have a lot of money.

RESULT

a. Many seniors retire near universities.

b. Americans are living longer.

c. Older Americans have the time and interest to exercise.

d. Ideas about beauty are changing too.

FROM READING TO WRITING

Reflecting on the Reading

Discuss the questions in pairs or small groups.

1. Is the population of your country getting older, as it is in the United States?
2. At what age do people retire in your country? What do people do after they retire in your country? For example, do they take university classes or exercise?
3. Do you agree that 50 is the new 30, and 70 the new 50? Why or why not?

Activating your Vocabulary

Complete the paragraph with the words from the box.

active	clients	healthy	population
average	experts	improve	retire

By the year 2030, (1) _____ say that 20 percent of
the (2) _____ of the United States will be over 65. And
the (3) _____ American will live to be 78 years old. What
are these older Americans like? Their doctors say that many of them
are very (4) _____ and have very (5) _____
activities. They exercise and take care of their bodies and minds.
Health club owners and personal trainers say that their older
(6) _____ enjoy the same sports and activities as
younger people. Also, many older Americans work. They do not
(7) _____. They want to continue working for as long as
they can. Many of them take classes at universities. They want to
(8) _____ their understanding of the world.

WRITING

Read the model paragraph.

MODEL

The average American family is changing. There are fewer children today
than in the past because many couples are choosing to have small families. There
are two main reasons for this. First of all, children cost a lot of money. Studies
show that the average cost of taking care of a child from birth to age 18 is about
$250,000 in the United States today. It is not a surprise, then, that some couples
cannot afford to have children. Second, both the husband and the wife work in
about 60 percent of American families, so they do not have time to take care of
children. Because Americans are having fewer children and people are living
longer, the average age of the American population is going up.

Using *because* and *so*

You have learned how to use **so** in a sentence to show the relationship between causes and results. You can also use **because** to write about causes and results, but notice that the ideas in the sentence are in a different order.

In a sentence with **so**, the **result** comes after the word *so*. In a sentence with **because**, the **cause** comes after the word *because*. Also, we use a **comma** in front of *so*, but we do not use a comma in front of *because*.

EXAMPLES

COMMA

┌────── CAUSE ──────┐ ┌── RESULT ──┐
- Americans take care of themselves, **so** they are living longer.

┌─── RESULT ───┐ ┌──── CAUSE ────┐
- Americans are living longer **because** they take care of themselves.

In sentences with **because**, we can put *because* at the **beginning** of the sentence or in the **middle**. If we put *because* at the beginning of the sentence, we put a **comma** between the cause and the result.

EXAMPLE

COMMA

┌────── CAUSE ──────┐ ┌── RESULT ──┐
- **Because** Americans take care of themselves, they are living longer.

Practice

A. Read the model paragraph again. Underline the sentences that contain so and because.

B. Rewrite each sentence using because in two ways. Keep the same meaning in all three sentences. Use a comma where necessary.

1. People are living longer, so there are more seniors.

   Because people are living longer, there are more seniors.

   There are more seniors because people are living longer.

2. Seniors want to stay active and healthy, so they exercise.

   _____

   _____

3. Many seniors want to take classes, so retirement communities near universities are popular.

_____

_____

4. Classes do not cost a lot of money, so most seniors can afford to take a class.

_____

_____

5. The seniors can make extra work for the professor, so some professors do not allow seniors to take their classes.

_____

_____

6. Seniors often study hard, so many professors welcome older students in their classes.

_____

_____

WRITING ASSIGNMENT

Write an opinion paragraph. Follow the steps.

STEP 1   **Get ideas.**

Choose a topic. (Topic 2 is on the next page.) Work in pairs. Ask and answer the questions. If you don't know a word, check your dictionary or ask someone the meaning.

❏ **Topic 1:** Families in my country

1. On average, how many children do couples in your country have today?
2. Is it expensive to have a child in your country today? For example, are clothes and food expensive? Are schools and universities expensive?
3. Is it common for both the husband and wife to work in your country? If so, who takes care of the children?
4. Is the average size of the family changing in your culture today? If so, why? If not, do you think it will change in the future? Explain your reasons.

❑ **Topic 2:** Senior citizens in my country

1. On average, how old do people live to be in your country today? Are people in your country living longer than in the past? If so, why do you think this is the case?
2. What is the average retirement age in your country?
3. What do people do after they retire?
4. In your opinion, do people in your country treat senior citizens well? Do they respect senior citizens? Why or why not?

STEP 2 **Write your paragraph.**

Complete one of the topic sentences below. Then use the topic sentence and information from your conversation with your partner to write your paragraph. Use some sentences with *because* and *so*.

❑ **Topic 1:** The average size of a family in my country today is _____.

❑ **Topic 2:** On average, people in my country today live to be about _____ years old.

STEP 3 **Check your work.**

Read your paragraph. Use the writing checklist to look for mistakes, and use the editing symbols on page 168 to mark corrections.

Writing Checklist
❑ Did you use *because* and *so* correctly?
❑ Did you use commas and periods correctly?
❑ Did you use correct paragraph form?

STEP 4 **Write a final copy.**

Correct your mistakes. Copy your final paragraph and give it to your instructor.

Millennials in the Workforce

In this chapter you will:

- read about a new generation of Americans

- learn about future time clauses and *if*-clauses

- write a paragraph about future plans

PRE-READING

Discussion

Discuss the questions in pairs or small groups.

1. Look at the picture. What are these young people doing?
2. Did you have a computer when you were a child? How old were you when you used a computer for the first time?
3. Did you use the Internet when you were a child? How old were you when you used the Internet for the first time?

Vocabulary

A. Read the sentences. Match the boldfaced words with the definitions in the box.

_____ 1. Work on the project together, not alone. **Share** your ideas with your co-workers.

_____ 2. She's famous. Her name is in the **media** almost every day. Yesterday, I saw her picture in the newspaper, on the Internet, and on television.

_____ 3. I want my children to **grow up** in the little town where my family lives.

_____ 4. Right now, my wife and I are living with her parents. It's difficult to live with people from another **generation**. We don't think the same way.

> a. the people in a society or family who are about the same age
> b. change gradually from being a child to being an adult
> c. television, radio, newspapers, and the Internet
> d. have or use something with someone else

B. Read the sentences. Match the boldfaced words with the definitions in the box.

_____ 1. He is a good player. He helps us win. He is a **valuable** member of the team.

_____ 2. Children need **structure** in their lives. For example, they need to wake up, eat, and go to bed at the same time every day.

_____ 3. Christina studied very hard for the test. She is **confident** that she will pass.

_____ 4. Our teacher is **fair**. She treats all of the students in the class the same.

> a. sure that you can do things well; not nervous
> b. dealing with people or situations in an equal way
> c. something that is organized carefully so that all the parts connect to make a whole
> d. very useful

Millennials in the Workforce

1   Can you remember a world before the Internet? If your answer is "no," then you are probably a millennial. Millennials are the new **generation** of young Americans. They were born between 1982 and 1992. There are 33 million of them, and they are just starting to enter the workforce.[1] Many experts believe that millennials are different from young Americans of past generations. They also believe that millenials will change the workforce in important ways.

2   How are millennials different? They are the first generation born in the computer age. The Internet has always been a part of their lives. They spend about 16 hours a week on the Internet, and this doesn't include e-mail. And they spend 72 hours a week using other electronic **media**, including cell phones and video games. They are "native speakers" of the language of the computer age. People who were born earlier will never be native speakers of that language. Why not? They did not **grow up** "speaking" it.

3   How will millennials change the workforce? To answer that question, it is important to understand how millennials use the Internet. They use the Internet to communicate. They visit websites such as FaceBook and MySpace every day. They **share** ideas, music, information, games, and friendships with people all over the world. When they start working, they will want to share their work and ideas with others.

4   It is also important to understand the way millennials grew up. Their parents and teachers gave them a lot of attention. They taught them that their opinions were **valuable**. As a result, many millennials are very **confident**. At work, they will expect their co-workers and bosses to listen to their opinions.

5   Millennials also grew up with a lot of **structure** in their lives. Many of them went to school from the age of two or three and played on sports teams. At work, they will expect the rules to be clear. They will also expect a strong but **fair** boss, like a coach[2] on a sports team. They will follow the person in charge if he or she is fair. But they will not follow an unfair boss. They will also expect their work to be fun and creative, similar to their experiences on a sports team.

6   These are a few of the changes that experts believe millennials will bring to the American workforce. But the world is changing very fast. There will probably be more changes that are difficult to imagine today.

---

[1] **workforce:** all of the people who work in a particular country or company
[2] **coach:** someone who trains people in a sport

Identifying Main Ideas

A. *What is the main idea of the reading? Underline the two sentences in the first paragraph that give the main idea.*

B. *Where could you add the sentences? Write 2 for paragraph 2, 3 for paragraph 3, and so on.*

_____ 1. They will not want to work alone.

_____ 2. They won't want to do boring work.

_____ 3. They will expect their older co-workers to listen to their ideas.

_____ 4. They do not remember a world before the Internet.

Identifying Details

Match the causes with the results.

CAUSE	RESULT
_____ 1. Their parents paid a lot of attention to them.	a. They expect to share ideas with others at work.
_____ 2. They grew up sharing music, information, and ideas with people from all over the world.	b. They are confident.
	c. They are comfortable using online media.
_____ 3. They played on sports teams.	d. They expect work to be fun.
_____ 4. They grew up using the Internet.	

FROM READING TO WRITING

Reflecting on the Reading

Discuss the questions in pairs or small groups.

1. How is your generation different from your parents' generation?
2. Are you a millennial? Why or why not?
3. Do you agree that millennials will change the workplace? Why or why not?

Activating your Vocabulary

Complete the sentences with the words from the box.

confident	generations	media	structure
fair	grows up	shares	valuable

1. They both do the same job, but he makes $10 an hour and she makes only $8 an hour. That isn't _____.

2. My sister is 15 years older than me. We are from different _____.

3. My daughter is six years old. She wants to be a doctor when she _____.

4. He never _____ his ideas. He always works alone.

5. When he retired, he was uncomfortable for a while because there was no _____ in his life. But now he enjoys having free time to do whatever he wants.

6. He is a _____ worker. We need him.

7. We didn't win the game because we weren't _____. We didn't think that we could win.

8. When he graduates, he wants to work in the news _____ as a writer for a newspaper or an online news organization.

WRITING

Read the model paragraph.

MODEL

> I feel confident about my future, but I'm a little nervous too. I am a senior in high school. When I graduate, my life will change forever. Choosing the correct college will be my first adult decision. Before I choose, I will find out as much information as I can. Right now, I am looking for information online about different colleges in the area. I will choose three or four colleges to apply to. I will visit them if they are not too far away. I think it's important to see them with my own eyes. After I finish my visits, I will relax and enjoy my last few months of high school.

WRITING SKILL

Using Future Time Clauses

You learned about past time clauses with *when*, *after*, and *before*. We also use time clauses to write about the **future**. In sentences with future time clauses, we use *will* + **simple form** of the verb in the **main clause**. In the **time clause**, we use the **present tense** of the verb. We do not use *will* in the time clause. If you start the sentence with the time clause, put a **comma** between the time clause and the main clause. If the main clause comes first, do not use a comma.

EXAMPLES

```
                    COMMA
┌── TIME CLAUSE ──┐ ┌──── MAIN CLAUSE────┐
```
• When I **graduate,** my life **will change** forever.
```
          │                    │
    PRESENT TENSE      WILL + SIMPLE FORM OF VERB
```

```
┌──── MAIN CLAUSE ────┐ ┌── TIME CLAUSE ──┐
```
• My life **will change** forever when I **graduate**.
```
          │                    │
WILL + SIMPLE FORM OF VERB    PRESENT TENSE
```

Practice

A. *Read the model paragraph again. Underline the time clauses.*

B. *Combine each pair of sentences to make one sentence with a time clause. Use commas where necessary. You will need to change the verb form in the time clause.*

1. She will go to college. She will live in a dormitory.

   When *she goes to college, she will live in a dormitory* .

2. She will move into the dormitory. School will start.

   She will move into the dormitory before *school starts* .

3. Classes will start. She will make new friends.

   Before _____ .

4. She will be very busy. Classes will start.

   _____ when _____ .

5. She will finish classes every day. She will go to the library.

   After _____ .

6. She will have a one-month vacation. The semester will end.

   _____ after _____ .

Using Clauses with *if*

We also use *if*-clauses to write about **future possibilities**. The
if-clause shows a condition, and the main clause shows the possible
future result of that condition.

As in a time clause, we use the **present tense** of the verb in the
if-clause, and *will* + **simple form** of verb in the **main clause**. We do
not use *will* in the *if*-clause. We use commas in the same way in *if*-
clauses and time clauses.

EXAMPLES

COMMA

┌— IF-CLAUSE (CONDITION) —┐ ┌——— MAIN CLAUSE (RESULT) ———┐
- If I **feel** comfortable, I **will apply** to that college.

PRESENT TENSE   WILL + SIMPLE FORM OF VERB

┌——— MAIN CLAUSE (RESULT) ———┐ ┌— IF-CLAUSE (CONDITION) —┐
- I **will apply** to that college if I **feel** comfortable.

WILL + SIMPLE FORM OF VERB   PRESENT TENSE

Practice

Combine each pair of sentences to make one sentence with an if-*clause.*
Use commas where necessary.

1. She won't like living in the dormitory. She will move to an
   apartment in town.

   <u>She will move to an apartment in town</u> if <u>she doesn't like</u>

   <u>living in the dormitory</u> .

2. She will study hard. She will get good grades.

   _____ if _____ .

3. She will get good grades. She will be happy.

   If _____ .

4. She will need money. She will get a part time job.

   If _____ .

5. She will feel lonely. She will call her parents.

   _____ if _____ .

6. She will make a lot of new friends. She won't feel lonely.

   If _____ .

Editing

Read the paragraph. Correct the comma and verb-form mistakes. There are six mistakes including the examples.

Six months before I graduate from college,^ I ^*will* start to look for a job. If I be lucky, I will find a job quickly. I will live at home with my parents, after I graduate. I will get my own apartment when I will save enough money. If the apartment is big, I will look for a roommate. After I work for a while, I will have enough money to buy a car. When I will have a job, an apartment, and a car, my life will be perfect!

WRITING ASSIGNMENT

Write a paragraph about your future plans. Follow the steps.

STEP 1   Get ideas.

Work in pairs. Ask and answer the questions. If you don't know a word, check your dictionary or ask someone the meaning.

1. How do you feel about your future? Confident? Nervous? Scared? Excited? Why do you feel that way?
2. What will you do when you finish this course? For example, will you take another English class? Look for a job?
3. What dreams do you have for the future? What will you do to make your dreams come true?

STEP 2   Write your paragraph.

Write a paragraph about your future plans. Use information from your conversation with your partner to complete the paragraph. Use some time clauses and some *if*-clauses.

I feel _____ about the future.

_____

_____

Right now, I _____

_____

When (*or* Before) _____

_____

_____

After _____

_____

_____

If _____

_____

_____

STEP 3   **Check your work.**

Read your paragraph. Use the writing checklist to look for mistakes, and use the editing symbols on page 168 to mark corrections.

Writing Checklist
❑ Did you use future time clauses correctly?
❑ Did you use *if*-clauses correctly?
❑ Did you use correct paragraph form?

STEP 4   **Write a final copy.**

Correct your mistakes. Copy your final paragraph and give it to your instructor.

Grammar Reference

A. Simple Present

The simple present is used to describe regular activities, facts, opinions, or ownership.

1. The Verb *be*

The simple present of *be* has three forms: *am, are, is*. In the negative, *not* comes after the verb.*

FORM/EXAMPLE	MEANING
I **am** always hungry in the morning. I **am not** hungry at noon if I eat a big breakfast.	A regular activity or habit
You **are** never late for breakfast. You **are not** late to lunch, either.	
We **are** almost ready to eat. We **are not** thirsty.	A fact
The bread **is** on the table. The coffee **is not** ready yet.	
The eggs **are** on the stove. The plates **are not** on the table.	

* Negative forms can be shortened: *I am not* = *I'm not. You are not* = *You're not* or *You aren't. We are not* = *We're not* or *We aren't. He is not* = *He's not* or *He isn't. They are not* = *They're not* or *They aren't.*

2. Other Verbs

The simple present of other verbs use the same form for all subjects except **he/she/it**.*

FORM/EXAMPLE	MEANING
Students often **sit** at outside tables to eat their lunch. Usually they **do not sit** on the benches.	A regular activity or habit
The cafeteria **has** excellent service. It **does not serve** pizza. The cook **takes** orders and **prepares** food quickly. The cook **does not talk** very much.	A fact
I **love** pancakes. I **do not like** toast.	An opinion or preference
You **prefer** coffee rather than tea. You **do not like** a cold drink in the morning.	
We **have** a nice, big kitchen for preparing meals. We **don't have** a table in our kitchen.	Ownership

* Negative forms with a *he/she/it* subject have **does not** (or **doesn't**) before the verb. Negative forms for other subjects have **do not** (or **don't**) before the verb.

B. Simple Past

The simple past is used to describe situations or activities that began and ended in the past.

1. The Verb *be*

The simple past of **be** has two forms: **was, were**. In the negative, **not** comes after the verb.*

FORM/EXAMPLE
I **was** very tired yesterday. I **wasn't** in a party mood.
You **were** a beautiful baby.
We **were** in the front row the last time.
The crowd **was** large.
The parents **were** happy, but their children **weren't**.

* Negative forms can be shortened: **was not** = **wasn't**, **were not** = **weren't**.

2. Regular Verbs

The simple past of regular verbs is formed by adding *-d* or *-ed* to the simple form of the verb. In the negative, ***did not*** (or ***didn't***) comes before the simple form of the verb.

FORM/EXAMPLE
I **loved** the party.
You **looked** very nice in your new suit.
We **enjoyed** holding the new babies. The babies **didn't cry** until the end of the day.
The food **tasted** delicious.
The guests **thanked** the parents for inviting them.

3. Irregular verbs

The simple past of irregular verbs have different forms. In the negative, ***did not*** (or ***didn't***) comes before the simple form of the verb.

FORM/EXAMPLE
I **ate** some cake, but I **didn't eat** anything else.
You **took** a lot of photos of the family.
We **spent** several hours at our friends' house.
Everyone **had** a chance to see all four babies together.
The babies **slept** through most of the party.

C. Simple Future

There are several ways to talk about future actions in English: one is to use *will*, another one is to use *be going to*.

1. *Will*

Will is used before the simple form of the verb.* In the negative, *will not* (or *won't*) are used.

FORM/EXAMPLE
I **will take** a vacation on a train across Canada next month. I **won't be** at work.
My vacation **will begin** on July 7, but the train **won't leave** my hometown until July 8.
We **will have** a sleeping car on the train. We **will not watch** one minute of television the whole time!

* This form can be shortened: *I will = I'll. We will = We'll.*

2. *Be going to*

Be going to is used before the simple form of the verb. In the negative, *not* comes after the form of *be*.*

FORM/EXAMPLE
I **am going to see** mountains, lakes, and animals from my train window. **I'm not going to think** about the city or my work.
You **are going to** miss me while I am gone. You **aren't going to be** lonely, are you?
We **are going to eat** all our meals on the train. We **aren't going to cook** or clean our rooms.
The train **is going to** travel across Canada. **It's not going to pick up** more passengers.
The train attendants **are going to tell** us about all the interesting sites along the way. They **aren't going to get** much rest during our trip.

* Negative forms can be shortened (see the simple present of *be*).

D. Imperative

The imperative is used to give commands, directions, advice, or requests.

The imperative is the simple form of the verb without a subject. "You" is the subject, but the word **you** is not included in the sentence. In the negative, **do not** (or **don't**) comes before the simple form of the verb.

FORM/EXAMPLE
Set your goals.
Don't forget them.
Be confident in yourself.
Don't be afraid.

E. Future Real Conditional

The future real conditional is used to explain what will happen under certain conditions. The *if* clause shows a condition, and the main clause shows the possible future result of that condition. In the *if* clause the present tense of the verb is used, and *will* + the simple present form is used in the main clause.

FORM/EXAMPLE
If it **rains**, **I'll stay** home.
I **will stay** home if it rains.

Punctuation and Capitalization

PUNCTUATION MARK	USE	EXAMPLE
.	Place a period at the end of a statement.	The Gauna family moved to New York last year.
?	Place a question mark at the end of a question.	How many children do Enrique and Andrea Gauna have?
!	Place an exclamation point at the end of a command or a statement that shows strong feeling.	They have six children. That's a lot!
,	Use a comma to indicate a short pause between ideas in a sentence. Follow the rules below. 1. Use commas to list three or more nouns, adjectives, verbs, or phrases. 2. Use commas before and after phrases that describe a person or thing. 3. Use a comma before a conjunction (*and, but, or, so*) that joins main clauses (clauses with a subject and verb) in a compound sentence. 4. Use a comma after a subordinate clause (a group of words that express only part of an idea and begins with *after, although, because, before, if, since, unless, until, when, while*).	On Friday, Saturday, and Sunday Andrea works from 8:00 to 5:00. Enrique, Andrea's husband, is from Puerto Rico. • Enrique has twin brothers, **and** he loves them very much. • Andrea wants to go to California for vacation, **but** Enrique wants to go to Florida. **Before** Andrea went to work, she took her children to school.

PUNCTUATION MARK	USE	EXAMPLE
" "	Use quotation marks to show the exact words that someone said or wrote.	Her son Julio said, "I have soccer practice after school today."
:	Use a colon before a list of items.	Julio plays three sports: soccer, baseball, and basketball.
;	Use a semicolon to separate two related clauses.	His sister Ana doesn't play any sports; she plays the piano.
'	Use an apostrophe in the situations below. 1. Use an apostrophe before or after *s* to show that something belongs or is related to someone. 2. Use an apostrophe to show that a letter has been left out in a contraction.	Andrea is driving Enrique**'s** truck today because her car won't start. She does**n't** like to drive his truck.
L	*Capitalize* means to begin a word with a capital letter. Capitalize words in the following situations: 1. Capitalize the first word of every sentence. 2. Capitalize the pronoun *I*. 3. Capitalize proper nouns (names of people, places, and things).	**T**hey love living in New York City. They like it, but **I** don't. I want to move to **S**eattle.

Editing Symbols

TO	USE THIS	EXAMPLE
add something	∧	We ate rice, bean, and corn.
delete something	ꝺ	We ate rice, beans, and corns
start a new paragraph	¶	¶We ate rice, beans, and corn.
add a comma	∧	We ate rice, beans and corn.
add a period	⊙	We ate rice, beans, and corn⊙
switch letters or words	∼	We ate rice, baehs, and corn.
change to a capital letter	ᴄ	we ate rice, beans, and corn.
change to a lowercase letter	⫽	WE ate rice, beans, and corn.

Target Vocabulary

*Coxhead's *Academic Word List* (2000)
**Dilin Liu's *The Most Frequently Used American English Idioms* (2003)

UNIT 1
(Chapters 1 & 2)

acceptable
agree
carefully
especially
expression
face
funny
in public
mistakes
notice
owe
relationship
respect
rules
touch
uncomfortable

UNIT 2
(Chapters 3 & 4)

arrive
beauty
characteristics
danger
famous
gift
hard
hide
kick
popular

protect
spend
spots
stranger
thick
welcome

UNIT 3
(Chapters 5 & 6)

attractive
burn
dessert
dish
fill
fortunately
meal
prevent
recipes
reheat
ripe
serve
spicy
sweet
taste
variety

UNIT 4
(Chapters 7 & 8)

advertisement
choose
customer

develop
guests
imagine
instead
make sure**
memorize
memory
method*
order
perfume
practice
products
useful

UNIT 5
(Chapters 9 & 10)

area*
community*
complete
crowded
design*
efficient
follow
housing
materials
own
residents*
separate
size
space
take care of**

UNIT 6	UNIT 7	UNIT 8
(Chapters 11 & 12)	*(Chapters 13 & 14)*	*(Chapters 15 & 16)*
a while	communicate*	active
actually	concern	average
allow	depend on	client
creative*	expect	confident
find out**	in charge**	expert*
graduate	interrupt	fair
heal	limit	generation*
nature	message	grow up**
nervous	negative*	healthy
operation	neutral*	improve
patients	patient	media*
project*	proud	population
refuse	reserved	retire
religion	tool	share
sensitive	voices	structure*
treatment	waste	valuable

Sources

The following are the sources used when researching the readings for *From Reading to Writing 1*.

UNIT 1, CHAPTER 1, The Land of Smiles

Holmes, Henry, and Suchada Tangtongtavy. *Working With the Thais: A Guide to Managing in Thailand*. Bangkok: White Lotus Co Ltd, 1997.

Fraser, Daniel. "Thai Smiles—Good, Bad, Ugly, and the 10 in between." 24 May 2007 <http://www.smilingalbino.com/blog/2006/05>

Pibulsonggram, Nitya. "Thailand: A Partner in Progress; A Land of Smiles." 25 Apr. 1996. 24 May 2007.
<http://www.thaiembdc.org/pressctr/statemnt/ambstmn/am042596.htm>

UNIT 2, CHAPTER 4, The Beautiful Stranger

Allin, Michael. *Zarafa: A Giraffe's True Story from Deep in Africa to the Heart of Paris*. New York: Walker and Company, 1998.

UNIT 4, CHAPTER 8, Smell, Memory, and Sales

Parker, Vicki Lee. "Businesses Sell Smells: Clients Pay for Scents to Improve Atmosphere, Sales." 3 Mar. 2006. 25 Aug. 2009.
<http://www.scentmarketing.org)>

Weiss, Tara. "Marketing Scents: The Smell of Money." *The Journal News*. 4 Sep. 2009.
<http://www.scribd.com/doc/8678773/Marketing-scents-The-smell-of-money>

UNIT 5, CHAPTER 10, The Micro-Compact Home

The information for the reading was obtained from the company's website at <http://www.microcompacthome.com/company/>

UNIT 6, CHAPTER 11, One Doctor, One Patient, Two Different Worlds

Grainger-Monsen, Maren. *Hold Your Breath*. Movie distributed by Fanlight Productions.

Rabinovitz, Jonathan. "Film Shows How Clash of Cultures Affects Treatment." *Stanford University News, Stanford Report*, 19 Jan. 2005. Webpage from Stanford School of Medicine, Stanford Center for Biomedical Ethics. 4 Sep. 2009.
<http://medethicsfilms.stanford.edu/holdyourbreath/about.html>

UNIT 6, CHAPTER 12, An Artist and a Doctor

Beggs Jr., Bill. "Artist Profile: Physician/Painter Is a True Renaissance Man." *Art Business News*. Jan. 2005. 25 Aug. 2009.
<http://www.fromearthtosky.com/>
<http://www.intlartandframing.com/aabn/january05/dept_profile.cfm>

UNIT 8, CHAPTER 15, Is 50 the New 30, and 70 the New 50?

Rosci, Frank. "Has '50' Become the New '30'?" Elkin, Michael. "Even a Sundance Kid Grows Up." *The Jewish Exponent*. 29 Jun. 2006. 25 Aug. 2009. <http://www.jewishexponent.com/article/3731/>

Photo Credits

Index

Writing

Complete sentences, 10, 18, 30, 38
Compound sentences with *and* and *but*, 50, 58
Compound sentences with *so* and *or*, 58
Paragraph about future plans, 158
Paragraph with *because* and *so*, 149
Paragraph with descriptive adjectives, 99
Paragraph with imperative sentences, 129
Paragraph with past and present tense, 78
Paragraph with prepositional phrases of time, 118
Paragraph with signal words of order, 138
Paragraph with *There is/There are*, 90
Paragraph with time clauses, 110
Sentences with correct capital letters, 38
Sentences with correct subject-verb agreement, 30
Sentences with subject and object pronouns, 70
Sentences with subject, verb, object, 18

Writing Skills

Formatting a paragraph, 56
Making subjects and verbs agree, 28
Replacing *There is/There are* with pronouns, 89
Using *because* and *so*, 148
Using capital letters, 37
Using clauses with *if*, 157
Using correct punctuation for sentences, 9
Using correct word order for a sentence, 17
Using descriptive adjectives, 97
Using future time clauses, 156
Using the imperative, 128
Using prepositional phrases of time, 117
Using present and past tense, 77
Using pronouns, 68
Using signal words, 136
Using *There is/There are*, 88
Using time clauses, 108
Using time words and expressions, 77
Writing a complete sentence, 8
Writing compound sentences with *and* and *but*, 48
Writing compound sentences with *so* and *or*, 57

Mechanics

Capital letters, 9, 37, 163
Commas, 48, 57, 108, 136, 148, 156, 157, 163
Periods, question marks, 9, 163
Editing Symbols, 164
Indenting, 56
Margins, 56

Grammar

Adjectives, 97
because and *so*, 148
Compound sentences, 48, 57
Future time clauses, 156
if-clauses, 157
Imperative, 128
Nouns and pronouns, 17
Prepositional phrases of time, 117
Proper nouns, 37
Singular/plural, 28
Subject/verb, 8, 28
Subject and object pronouns, 17, 65, 68
Subject/verb/object, 17
There is/There are, 88, 89
Time clauses (*before* and *after*), 106, 108

Readings

The Art of Food, 54
An Artist and a Doctor, 114
The Beautiful Stranger, 34
Cohousing, 84
Cultural Rules, 4
Doing Business in the United Kingdom, 124
E-Mail: Terrific Tool or Time-Waster? 133
Four Animals or One? 24

Is 50 the New 30, and 70 the New 50? 142

The Land of Smiles, 14

Memory Methods, 64

The Micro-Compact Home, 94

Millennials in the Workforce, 153

One Doctor, One Patient, Two Different Worlds, 104

Science in the Kitchen, 44

Smell, Memory, and Sales, 74

Reading Skills

Finding supporting sentences, 46

Finding the topic of a paragraph, 5

Identifying Details, 5, 14, 25, 35, 45, 55, 65, 75, 85, 95, 105, 115, 125, 134, 145, 154

Identifying Main Ideas, 5, 14, 25, 34, 45, 55, 65, 75, 85, 95, 105, 115, 125, 134, 145, 154

Identifying topic sentences, 85

Understanding cause and effect, 146

Understanding pronoun reference, 65

Understanding signal words, 126

Understanding time order, 106

Discussion

2, 12, 22, 32, 42, 52, 62, 72, 82, 92, 102, 112, 122, 131, 142, 151

Vocabulary

3, 7, 13, 16, 23, 28, 33, 36, 43, 47, 53, 56, 63, 67, 73, 76, 83, 87, 93, 96, 103, 107, 113, 116, 123, 127, 132, 135, 143, 147, 152, 155